# Gender, Power and Organisation

Women in western society have entered the workplace in increasing numbers only since the 1950s, and this entry has been rapid. *Gender, Power and Organisation* is an examination of the psychological impact of the work setting on professional women, which has become a major site of gender politics over the last twenty years. This book, however, is not primarily about the political and social challenge of inequality of numbers, but about the psychological consequences of this gender imbalance for senior and middle ranking women in management and the professions.

Paula Nicolson re-examines the ways that patriarchal structures resist women's progress, and how male success has psychological implications for women's sense of subjectivity, self-esteem and gender identity, and how achieving against such odds has an impact on women's everyday lives.

*Gender, Power and Organisation* is particularly concerned with women who have achieved or aspire to professional power, and the psychological dimension of power for women, men and the organisations in which they work.

**Paula Nicolson** is Lecturer in Psychology at the University of Sheffield Medical School, and has co-edited a number of books including *Gender Issues in Clinical Psychology, The Psychology of Women's Health and Health Care* (both with Jane Ussher) and *Female Sexuality: Psychology, Biology and Social Context* (with Precilla Choi).

# Gender, Power and Organisation

A psychological perspective

Paula Nicolson

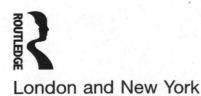

London and New York

First published 1996
by Routledge
11 New Fetter Lane, London EC4P 4EE

Simultaneously published in the USA and Canada
by Routledge
29 West 35th Street, New York, NY 10001

*Routledge is an International Thomson Publishing company*

Typeset in Baskerville by Routledge
Printed and bound in Great Britain by
TJ Press (Padstow) Ltd, Padstow, Cornwall

*British Library Cataloguing in Publication Data*
*A catalogue record for this book is available from the British Library*

*Library of Congress Cataloguing in Publication Data*
Nicolson, Paula.
     Gender, power and organization: a psychological perspective/
Paula Nicolson.
     Includes bibliographical references and index.
     1. Women in the professions – Psychological aspects.
     2. Sex role in the work environment.
     3. Professional socialization.     I. Title.
  HD6054.N53     1996
  155.6′ 33–dc20  95–51514 CIP

ISBN 0–415–10402–5 (hbk)
ISBN 0–415–10403–3 (pbk)

*To Kate Nicolson*

# Contents

# Acknowledgements

Caroline Dryden persuaded me to submit the proposal for this book during a conversation in a crowded pub, and now the book is finished I would like to thank her. Sue Walsh eventually convinced me of the importance of psychoanalytic insights into the relationship of gender to power, and we have had some interesting arguments to that end.

They and many others provided stimulation and support during the intervening years as I wrote and rewrote the manuscript. They include Jane Ussher and Jan Burns, other colleagues and friends in the Psychology of Women Section, the Universities of East London and Sheffield, the legal profession and the National Health Service.

I would specifically like to mention Bipasha Ahmed, Kay Barnes, Dorothy Birks, Jill Brunt, Precilla Choi, Kathleen Cox, Kathy Doherty, Janet Kells, Sian Lewis, Kate McKenzie Davey, Glenys Parry, Anna Thomasson, Jill Tunaley, Sharon Wallach, Christopher Welsh and Anne Woollett. Thanks also goes to Viv Ward at Routledge for her support and patience.

Finally, I wish to acknowledge the late Barrie Newman (who gave me invaluable insights into relevant aspects of sociology, although I am not so sure he would have really liked what I have made of it all); Derry Nicolson, who organised our entire house move whilst I finished this book; and Sue Thorpe and Richard Alderslade, who were there, both on e-mail and in person, while I was writing the last draft.

# Introduction

At any given moment, gender will reflect the material interests of those who have power and those who do not.

(Brittan, 1989: 3)

Organisational processes are central to the understanding of gender relations, and ... organisations are gendered.

(Witz and Savage, 1992: 3)

The power dynamics inherent in traditional conceptualisations of gender was theorised in the writings of those who noted that 'difference' was often equated with women's subordination or inadequacy

(Radtke and Stam, 1994: 5)

Both gender relations and organisational dynamics are about the achievement and maintenance of power. The ability to influence and control human and material resources exists in a social and relational context where power and subordination are inseparable. This alliance occurs in professional organisations, and sexual, social and family relationships. It is almost always the case that women are in some way subordinate in these contexts (Leonard, 1984; Bleier, 1984).

This project is an examination of the psychological impact of the work setting on professional women, currently entering organisations in increasing numbers. It is particularly concerned with women who have achieved or aspire to professional power, and expressly about the *psychological* dimension of power for women, men and the organisations in which they work.

Work organisations have become a major site of gender politics for professional women and men over the last twenty years. While equal opportunities policies and affirmative action in the selection and training of women in the professions and management have had a qualified impact (Aitkenhead and Liff, 1990); increased career opportunities appear to have made the psychological context of the organisation more stressful for women (Davidson and Cooper, 1992; Marshall, 1984; McKenzie Davey, 1993).

What makes this the case? While women and men have always co-existed in various capacities in extended families, their relationships in the workplace are relatively new. Women in western society have been entering the workplace in increasing numbers since the late 1950s, and this entry has been rapid. By 1975 46.2 per cent of women in OECD[1] countries were working outside the home for a wage. This pattern is set to continue. In the UK it is predicted that 75 per cent of women will be working by 2001 (Commission of the European Communities, 1990, quoted in Davidson and Cooper, 1993). However this has not been, and is unlikely to be, on equal or gender-free terms. Female work is typically part-time and in low status occupations, such as clerical, secretarial, nursing, health care, teaching, child-care and social work, sales and manufacturing (OECD, 1979). These occupations have provided some opportunity for professional career progression, but men who enter these professions consistently rise to the top relatively quickly while women remain in the junior posts (Reskin and Padavic, 1994). There is also a persistent, close relationship between relatively low pay and 'typically female' occupations such as teaching and nursing (Pillinger, 1993).

Although men have traditionally succeeded over women in terms of their pay, seniority and status of their profession, women are now entering the preservations of male power, such as politics, management, and professions such as medicine, law, academia and accountancy, but the picture is far from one of equality.

In the medical profession, for example, while women have trained as doctors in increasing numbers since the 1970s, there is little change in their proportions at the top of the profession in either the UK or USA (Silver, 1990; Department of Health, 1991–2). Within the branches of the profession where status and remuneration are high (e.g. surgery) only 3 per cent of consultants are women; while in psychiatry, where the patient group and opportunities for lucrative private practice in the UK are low, around 25 per cent are female (Department of Health, 1991–2). Even so, most are men.

Women academics are about seven times more likely to be temporary contract researchers than they are to be professors; and even then women only comprise around 35 per cent of contract researchers, 15 per cent of lecturers, 6 per cent of senior lecturers and 4 per cent of professors (AUT, 1990).

In the USA 35–50 per cent of all new employees in public accounting are women (Lehman, 1990) but only around 2 per cent achieve the status of senior partner in prestigious companies (Maupin, 1993).

The legal profession in the USA and UK demonstrates a similar pattern, with only 3.6 per cent of women in the UK being High Court judges (Holland and Spencer, 1992).

In the USA only one half of 1 per cent of top people in the highest category of management are women (Fierman, 1990) and there are similar figures for female chief executives in the UK (Davidson and Cooper, 1992).

This book, however, is not primarily about the identification and political and social challenge of inequality of numbers. This contest has been taken up effectively elsewhere (e.g. Hansard Society Commission, 1990; Davidson and Cooper, 1992). It is about the *psychological consequences* of this gender imbalance for senior and ambitious middle ranking women in management and the professions (Marshall, 1984; White et al., 1992).

What happens to women who distinguish themselves in their organisations? Successful and aspiring women appear to differ from others in several ways. They differ from their peers who enter the professions but who are sidetracked or who drop out. They are separated from women who choose not to enter professional life in the first place but opt for the more traditional family/non-career employment route. They differ from those women who choose semi-professional administration or secretarial/personal assistant work. Most significant is that they are unlike their main work peers who are men. These differences have major psychological consequences. There are few role models to provide inspiration, not only at work, but in all aspects of life.

[In this book I re-examine the ways that patriarchal structures resist women's progress; how male success has psychological implications for women's experiences in terms of their sense of subjectivity and self-esteem, their perceptions of their own and other women's femininity and gender identity, and the impact of these issues on their physical and emotional health; and how achieving against such odds has an impact on women's everyday life.

The general theme is not new (see Marshall, 1984; McKenzie Davey, 1993) but nevertheless neglected, and the more opportunities there are for women to achieve, the more scrutiny women's *experience* of career accomplishment is required so that success may be sustained.

In 1971 DeLameter and Fidell wrote about the problems of professional women as having a 'cumulative impact... as she moves from childhood to occupational employment' (Fidell and DeLameter, 1971: 7). They suggested how girls are socialised into being people-oriented and dependent, while work, and particularly success at work, was perceived to be masculine, and as such undesirable for women. They suggest that 'socialisation to traditional feminine values results in lower occupational aspirations for women' (Fidell and DeLameter, 1971: 7). Their edited collection demonstrated that the end of the 1960s had brought an awareness of gender and power as issues for social science. What has changed since then is that many women's aspirations have been raised. However, the conflicts and contradictions inherent in women's lives, subjectivities/identities and experiences as professionals in patriarchal organisations, have taken on a similar pattern to that reported thirty years before. There are still psychological, social and structural barriers to women's career success (Hansard Society Commission, 1990). The Hansard report argued that women

> face general barriers which transcend differences of occupation and sector – out-dated attitudes towards women's roles in society, sex discrimination, inadequate provision of child care facilities or support for the care of elderly dependants, and inflexibility in the organisation of work and careers.
>
> (Hansard Society Commission, 1990: 20)

These barriers have a psychological impact, and women pay the price, either in loss of career potential, or in more personal ways. This is different from the experience of men. While by no means all ambitious men succeed, the majority of people who do succeed are men. The personal and professional costs of career failure are recognised as attacking masculine identity, but there is little theorisation of the influence of career success or failure on feminine identity. Masculinity is equivalent to success, achievement and power, while femininity is largely still perceived by men and women in the outdated, traditional way as dependent passivity. This has implications for self-esteem, gender relations at home and at work, and is critical for women who challenge traditional gender expectations. Thus, although the potential cost of thwarted ambition is painful for men, and may skew their own self-evaluation, the lack of a similar career-expectation model for women denies them a framework through which to explain their experiences and emotions to themselves and others. A woman who fails to achieve promotion or appointment to a senior management post or to become a judge is seen – and, to some extent, probably sees herself – as lucky to get that far. This is particularly problematic because of the way women have to struggle for their success and have to develop intricate coping and image management strategies that appear to be essential to organisational achievement (see Marshall, 1984; Cassell and Walsh, 1991).

My interest in this particular aspect of organisational psychology arose from personal experience. As an academic, feminist and psychologist, taking up a post at a medical school in a psychiatry department I experienced extreme culture shock. Following life in a psychology department with its share of strong female and male colleagues, I was suddenly an outsider: not a man but a woman, not a psychiatrist but a psychologist, not interested in experimental research but with research interests in non-traditional areas.

There seemed to have been no precedent. Women were expected to be seen, work hard and definitely not heard. If they were not prepared or unable to fit this template there seemed to be no end to the hostility and envy. I was appointed to a reasonably junior position, and thus could afford to avoid a high-profile presence. I wondered how much worse the feelings of hostility might have been if I had arrived as head of the department.

The experience made me contemplate the practical, day-to-day aspects of the relationship between psychology, power and subordination in organisations. How do women cope as outsiders? What survival strategies do they need to adopt? Where do they find allies when their immediate context is populated by obstructive men (and no doubt in some cases obstructive women)? How does this effect women as they rise through the hierarchy? How can women avoid selling out? What are women's responsibilities towards other women? I came to recognise that the psychological survival of women in organisations is a key issue for feminist psychology.

The material for this book is not based on a single research project but has emerged from a range of sources. Initially my experience of culture shock gave rise to discussion with friends, all of whom in different ways recognised similar experiences to my own. Although few of us worked in the same cities, we had (and continue to have) an unwritten agreement to be available on the end of the phone (and nowadays e-mail) as soon as possible to discuss organisational issues which are precipitating problems. These appear to be almost exclusively related to gender issues on some level, and have provided essential food for thought.

As a consequence of my 'self' interest, I have given serious attention to women and professional power over the last few years. I became involved in providing supervision/consultancy to individuals and groups of women in senior posts in male dominated professions. This frequently involves detailed discussion of the stresses and strains of everyday working life, and although not all of these are directly attributable to gender discrimination as such, they are attributable to the fact that women are in the minority, that they do not have a long tradition of networking and mentoring other women, that they feel isolated but are not always prepared to admit it, and that women's *lives* (rather than their biological and psychological make-up) on the whole do not prepare them for senior professional and managerial roles.

I conducted a series of interviews for *The Independent* (a national British newspaper) with outstanding female lawyers, whose words and deeds provided a source of thought and inspiration. Also, a key component of my academic research, with a colleague Chris Welsh, has been to examine gender discrimination and sexual harassment, in medical school and in clinical settings, for medical students and doctors. We observed the strategies for survival that women had to adopt as they rose up the medical hierarchy, which involved distancing themselves from junior women and from problems of sexism, and moving towards an individualised sense of responsibility for achievement and combating sexism (see Nicolson and Welsh, 1993). These findings persuaded me to concentrate on the psychological consequences for women of the need to achieve success, rather than the experience of the forces of discrimination at the start of a career.

Finally, I have had the benefit of being able to draw upon the work of those who have conducted research and written about gender and career before me. Their work is wide ranging, covering home–work conflict, coping with sexism, the development of coping strategies, organisational culture and unconscious aspects of organisational and interpersonal life. Extracts from their interviews as well as the authors' own analysis of the importance of these extracts have been invaluable in mapping out the arena within which women's experiences may be understood (see, for instance, the work of Beverly Alimo-Metcalfe, Cary Cooper, Marilyn Davidson, Ginny Dougary, Jenny Firth-Cozens, Wendy Hollway, Judi Marshall, Jane McLoughlin, Celia Morris, Barbara White and others mentioned below in what follows).

I have divided the book into three main parts, which are not mutually exclusive. Part I, 'Biography, biology and career', sets out the core theoretical framework which develops a critical position towards tradi-tional, positivist academic psychology's contribution to career and organisation. I argue, first, for a feminist perspective on understanding the lives and experiences of women; second, I develop a social construc-tionist/biographical framework which originates from the work of sociologists to explain the impact of career success and failure on subjectivity/identity and self-esteem; and third, I take a psychoanalytic/ post-modern perspective for deconstructing what counts as human knowledge.

Part II, 'Professional socialisation and patriarchal culture', explores the ways in which femininity and masculinity are acted out at work on both a conscious and unconscious level. This includes the means by which stereotypes are employed to disadvantage women, particularly in terms of home vs. work priorities, leadership characteristics and the development and failure of support networks for women and men. It focuses upon the importance of envy and competition in work organisations and shows how this often sets men against women to the disadvantage of women. Finally, the enduring theme of sexuality and professional life is explored.

In Part III, 'Challenging patriarchy: No Man's Land?', I return to earlier themes, although I shift from the critique of the status quo to the examination of solutions. The role of feminism for understanding organisational life is discussed, particularly in terms of understanding the meaning and consequences of success and power for women and men. The importance of defining and negotiating boundaries for understanding the management of survival strategies is emphasised, and finally a model for women's mutual criticism and support is discussed.

## NOTE

1 The Organization for Economic Co-operation and Development was set up in 1960. Participating countries included USA, UK, Canada and many western European countries.

# Part I

# Biography, biology and career

# Introduction to Part I

This book develops a feminist critique of traditional psychology, implicitly and explicitly. Implicitly, because the book is about women, and their relationships with other women and men within patriarchal organisations. Gender relations are not characteristically the focal point of academic psychology (Woolett et al., 1995). Explicitly, because it challenges conventional psychological approaches to development in adulthood, gender identity and sex roles inasmuch as they retain the concept of the unitary individual as the focus. I argue, along with many social and feminist psychologists and sociologists, that this is unhelpful both in theorising gender–power relations and in understanding the organisational context in which these relationships are played out (Hollway, 1989).

Following Harré et al. (1985), contemporary psychology makes the assumptions that 'each person is a psychological unit in which all important processes occur' (1985: 2). Therefore 'causes' and 'consequences' of individual development are somehow predictable and observable in the individual. Thus, thinking, emotion and gender identity for each of us is taken to be the legacy of our biology – and social context – circumscribed within the boundary of the physical body.

There is also a tendency in academic psychology towards assuming the results of studies 'of the people of one's own "tribe" are true of all others' (Harré et al., 1985: 2). This has meant that psychological 'knowledge' based upon the behaviour of white, male, North American college students until relatively recently has been seen to be unproblematic and inconsequential (see Geertz, 1979, quoted in Sampson 1989: 1). It has meant that the behaviour and performance of this group has been taken as the normative 'baseline' by which others have been measured, thus creating inadequate and pathological groups (Broverman et al., 1970; Nicolson, 1995a; Ussher, 1989, 1992a, b). Feminist psychologists have also made this point forcefully, in relation to class and ethnicity (see, for example, Reinhartz, 1985; Bhavnani and Phoenix, 1994).

Psychology's apparent unquestioning assumption of individualism has not eluded dispute from a number of sources within and outside the discipline (e.g. Harré and Gillett, 1994; *Changing The Subject*, 1984; Potter and Wetherell, 1987). Neither has the priority given to men and male behaviour as the norm escaped challenge (Henwood and Pidgeon, 1995; Reinhartz, 1985). However, response to these challenges has not led to significant shifts in approach to substance or method in psychology.

Feminist influence in social science has inspired like-minded psychologists, aware that their own discipline has sadly lagged behind sociology, anthropology, human geography and social history (Wilkinson, 1986). Feminist psychologists draw upon feminist theories and methods which overall have been critical of positivism, particularly its requirements for the measurement of observable behaviour and the experimental approach (Reinhartz, 1985), the focus on the unitary subject as the locus of study (Hollway, 1989), and the reliance on male defined norms as the basis for what counts as knowledge (Ussher, 1989).

Over the past ten years in particular, feminist and social psychologists have begun to take qualitative approaches to research seriously. While there is no intrinsic reason why qualitative research is 'more feminist' than quantitative research (indeed Celia Kitzinger, 1990, has argued that qualitative approaches have been used to pathologise lesbians), the persuasive case has been made for qualitative research as conducive to developing knowledge that takes account of the contradictions and conflicts in women's lives (Stanley and Wise, 1983; Wilkinson, 1984; Lewis, 1995; Tunaley, 1995).

One influential development for academic feminists in psychology has been discourse analysis, which is a technique of data collection and analysis with its roots in post-modern critiques of science and knowledge. It prioritises language and power as central to cultural reproduction and to all areas of life. This technique has been explained and operationalised to examine key feminist issues, and has led to the knowledge that:

> prejudice towards women, personal identity and even deeply felt emotions like jealousy are not things hiding inside the person which a psychologist can then 'discover' but are created by the language that is used to describe them. Psychological phenomena have a public and collective reality, and we are mistaken if we think that they have their origin in the private space of the individual.
>
> (Burman and Parker, 1993: 1)

It is easy to see how such an approach is valuable to feminists. Post-modern critiques and applications of discourse analysis enable the identification of linguistic repertoires and exposure of structural power relations under patriarchy (Wetherell, 1993). Also, an emphasis on language and power in discourse accounts for the continuity and contradictions in human interactions and emotion (Weedon, 1987). In the process of deconstructing the 'subject-as-agent and the unitary individual . . . it provides a critique which gets underneath what is taken for granted by those terms' (Hollway, 1989: 31).

It is also significant to see how some feminists have found this approach to gender–power relations to be unacceptable. This is in part because it is potentially 'marginalising' for those who fail to accept the deconstructionist orthodoxy, but, more importantly, because of the possibility of depoliticisation in the conceptualisation and reification/celebration of sexual difference (Burman, 1989). (See chapters 3 and 6 for examples of this.)

While the impact of post-modern theory and practice has been debated thus among feminists in psychology (Burman, 1990b) there has been less said about understanding women's experience of self/subjectivity (see Changing the Subject, 1984; Hollway, 1989), and many would see notions of discourse and individual meaning and experience as inherently and irrefutably contradictory and thus incompatible (see, for example, Wetherell, 1993).

However, recently this orthodoxy has been called to account within social psychology. Questions have been raised about the complex tension between a post-modern approach to gender–power relations and the personal experience of subjectivity. My belief is that to exclude a *sense of the individual* from critical and feminist psychology is unproductive in the long term, and increases the widening gap between feminist psychologists and the women who might benefit from their analysis of gender–power relations (Doherty, 1994; Dryden, in press; Lewis, 1994; Tunaley, 1994; Nicolson 1994a). However, I do not want to throw the baby out with the bathwater! The theory and practice of discourse analysis has been exceptional in denting the positivist barriers of academic psychology, but is itself in danger of losing its grounding in everyday life (see Lewis, 1995).

A major task of this book, which examines the lives and careers of professional women, is to *contextualise experience* as one of dynamic and ongoing interaction between discourses of gender and power, and the experience and meaning of being an individual in a social context (see Nicolson, 1994a). This is particularly salient when there is conflict and contradiction between the experience of being a woman and the social construction of femininity, which explicitly prioritises the non-assertive and non-rational part of human action and emotion (see Broverman et al., 1970; Bem, 1974; Nicolson, 1992a).

The dilemma for many professional women is how to negotiate and give meaning to their sense of femininity and gender identity in the world of power and intellect, when that world has defined them out. It may be summarised thus:

> Bearers of the heritage of the 'Age of Reason' as we are, it can be argued that it is fundamentally contradictory for us in the West to think about women as rational or to perceive them as askers of questions or thinkers. Nor do these images fit the views and stereotypes about traditional femininity. The basic question is: how do feminine identity and intellectual thinking go together?
>
> (Wager, 1995: 2)

In what follows I argue the case for women to (re)claim their right to the world of intellect, authority and power which is denied them under current social practices which position the normal woman as emotional, nurturing and passive, with the difficult, unfeminine harridan as disturbing the boundaries around the rightful territory of men. It is stressful to be seen as marginal to patriarchy, and the successful woman is marginalised because she is unfeminine and as a consequence of having to 'toughen herself up' to get anywhere against the existing male strongholds.

In this first part of the book, the interrelationship between the gendered social context and the developing individual is explored. It is argued that although the identification of social discourses and gender–power relations is crucial to understanding women's lives, it is equally important to acknowledge experience of an 'inside' or 'interior' subjectivity expressed as the 'self' or 'identity'. Identity comprises both a sense of continuity and of disorder (see, for instance, Marris, 1986; Nicolson, 1988) and although it is constrained by both language/discourse and biology/sex, it is not simply the product of either.

All individuals are born into the social structures of pre-existing societies (Leonard, 1984) where gender is an important means of demarcation and stratification (Bleier, 1984) and are socialised through contact with family, peers, educational and political institutions.

All individuals exist in some relation to their social context so that being comfortable with ones' own gender is a prerequisite for emotional health. However, being an ambitious and successful woman is inimical to femininity. To struggle, fight, succeed or fail in the world of business, management or the professions is not something women typically do because it is not part of their sex role socialisation. When women do fight to succeed and whether or not they achieve what they wish, they more or less do so alone, because despite increased numbers of women at or near the top, they are still in the minority.

In Chapter 1, 'Gender, subjectivity and feminism', I make the case to distinguish and privilege feminist psychology over positivist psychology. I begin by examining the meaning of gender and gendered behaviour for human psychology, reiterating the feminist argument that women have been marginalised and made deficient through what counts as psychological knowledge.

In Chapter 2, 'Gender, knowledge and career', I examine the relationship between psychological development in adulthood as it occurs in the context of the profession/organisation. This is achieved specifically from the perspective of biography as a reflexive enterprise, where the person actively participates and reflects upon their developing identity/subjectivity. For this I identify and draw on the work of George Herbert Mead and subsequent writers on symbolic interactionism and phenomenology (in particular Peter Berger), as well as the contemporary sociologist Anthony Giddens and writers on social psychology such as Rome Harré and John Shotter. The emphasis is upon the way subjectivity, biography and meaning are constructed and reconstructed through language in thought and conversation. For successful and aspiring career women, biography is about struggle, change and potential failure. For the equivalent group of men, it is more about the means of achievement. Thus failure and success need to be re-evaluated in relation to human identity/subjectivity and women's experiences should not be neglected.

Chapter 3, 'Femininity, masculinity and organisation', examines the way that women and men differ in terms of the meaning given to their bodies and gender identity and how this impacts upon their career and organisational relationships. It examines what is meant by masculinity and femininity and the relation between the two. Psychoanalytic ideas from Freud to Lacan are explored, as well as the commentary and analysis of writers such as Teresa Brennan, Juliet Mitchell, Janet Sayers and Stephen Frosh.

# Chapter 1

# Gender, subjectivity and feminism

## SEX, GENDER AND THE PSYCHOLOGY OF WOMEN

Make no mistake about it, the role is meant to be performed. Sex roles are no theoretical fiction concocted by psychologists or sociologists or even by militant feminists. They have just baptised a creature that women have always been able to delineate. When asked, women can describe the dimensions of their own sex role. What is more, they can describe the punishments incurred for any infringements: the emotional blackmail and social shame.

(Breakwell, 1985: 2)

This chapter explores definitions of sex, gender and gender relations, and their implications for women's professional lives. To accomplish this, I examine the complex relationship between science, popular knowledge and women's experience and behaviour; particularly the way women are positioned, and position themselves, as 'feminine', 'powerful' and 'autonomous' – traditionally contradictory positions within a patriarchal context.

Sex, sex roles and gender are related concepts, but each requires definition and explanation for the part they play in the construction of gender relations and subjectivity/identity.

### Sex

Social, biological and psychological influences on our lives come together in a complex way in relation to *sex*. Differences between the way women and men experience these competing and complementary forces are emphasised in both scientific literature and in everyday life, where they are taken for granted and frequently characterised as the 'battle between the sexes'. But why does designated sex appear to make so much difference to the life-course of individuals? Why are women punished for stepping outside the boundaries of recognised sex roles? How does sex and sexuality influence professional relationships?

Most of us are born either female or male and that designation is called our 'sex', which is initially dependent upon genetic endowment, and subsequent characteristics depend upon hormone distribution prior to birth and at various stages of the life cycle. Biological and anatomical differences between women and men are strikingly visible. Female and male bodies have much in common that makes them both human, but they are also different in incisive ways, specifically in connection with their reproductive organs.

The physical characteristics of females and males represent clear anatomical distinctions: − body fat and hair distribution, reproductive functions and genitals (Archer and Lloyd, 1982). However, the anatomical distinctions are not simplistic. They represent social and ideological constraints as well as biological ones.

## Gender

*Gender* is different from sex in that it refers to the *social* characteristics whereby women and men exist in a dynamic structural relation to each other. Although biologically designated, sex has a significant part to play in the way human experience is defined; that explication is subject to layers of psychological experience mediated by personality, socialisation, sexuality and gender divisions, which are themselves socially constructed.

Gender, then, is a *process* through which social life is organised at the level of the individual, family and society (Connell, 1993). This means it is also crucial in the structure of organisations. It prescribes and defines the parameters of individual human experience in that women's lives are different from men's (Rohrbaugh, 1981; Nicolson, 1992a), and through the recognition that individuals are in possession of a gendered self or subjectivity through which they themselves interpret their own experiences and operate constraints (Hollway, 1989).

Anatomy, as well as embodiment, is characterised by the ways women and men *use* their bodies to express everyday femininity and masculinity and experience sexual sensation. For example, we emphasise our physical shape, and attributes which have been socially defined as attractive to sexual partners, through dress, hairstyle, posture, make-up and physical movement. The result is that women's passive/responsive qualities are emphasised − as are men's potentially aggressive/active ones (see Chapter 3).

Anatomy/biology has a clearly social meaning encapsulated in the discourses on gendered behaviour (Sayers, 1986), so that when we look at a woman, the female body symbolises an entire 'social history' through which others can understand her and through which she makes sense of her own life (Ussher, 1989).

Anatomy provides a set of physical symbols through which sex and gender, meanings and representations are communicated. The social meanings given to anatomical symbols operate in a deterministic way so that whether the argument is based upon biological, social or psychological factors, anatomy *is* destiny (Nicolson, 1994b).

It is this idea of destiny that is intriguing and especially important here. While the notion that social meanings are attributed to biology is far from reductionist in perspective, it may still be seen as deterministic in that social ideas about sex, gender and sexuality are neatly bound up in the concept of female reproductive life. When we see a woman we assume certain personality traits, certain behaviours, certain limits to her experience and, most importantly, we see her in some relation to motherhood rather than professional success (Nicolson 1992b, 1993a). Women's biological capacities to bear and feed children are presented in patriarchal societies as the determining features of what is 'natural', and conversely what is 'unnatural'. Childlessness and traits contrary to the nurturing role, such as aspiring to and achieving social power, are presented as unfeminine and somehow 'damaging' to potential femininity (Ehrenreich and English, 1979).

## Gender relations

Gender relations are *power* relations, through which men and male values have superordinate status over women and female values, and socialisation into gender roles is an integral part of the maintenance of the patriarchal power structure (Leonard, 1984; Hollway, 1989). Women and men experience their worlds through these contextualised relationships, and therefore it is arguably the role of academic psychology to explore their psychologies *within the gendered context*. However, scientific knowledge reflects a value system that not only fails to tackle effectively the disadvantages in women's lives but, through its knowledge claims, privileges male experience over female. Thus most of what counts as legitimate psychological knowledge mirrors this privilege (for instance, in relation to cognition and the menstrual cycle, where despite critique and contrary research evidence, researchers continue to investigate women's cognitive problems during the pre-menstrual period) (Ussher, 1992b).

All women are positioned, and position themselves, within the discourse on female reproduction and associated 'qualities', and although femininity itself is arguably less prescribed than masculinity, which is defined through 'what it is not' (Archer, 1989; and see Chapter 4), femininity is constantly regulated through patriarchal exploitation of the intrinsic relationship between reproductive function and acceptable womanhood. Feminine women have to behave in what are deemed socially appropriate ways.

## Sex roles

Sex roles represent an intricate pattern of involvement between sex, gender and everyday experience. Women and men have expectations placed upon them from a range of constituents, identified collectively as 'society'. These include parents, the family, peers and institutions such as school, university, religious bodies and work organisations. However, these expectations are neither easy nor comfortable to fulfil, nor are they value free (Breakwell, 1985). To 'become' a girl/woman and to 'become' a boy/man cannot be left to biology alone (Archer, 1989). Women and men have to learn what is expected of their sex; they also have to negotiate with themselves and their immediate social context what it is possible and desirable to do as members of each sex.

Further, sex differences are not neutral categories. As Leonard (1984) argues, entry into the social order for females means that they are 'from the start expected to defer to males, to accept the leadership of males, to be in a word, subordinate'. Women, as a consequence of gender–power relations then, are more likely to accept the patriarchal/male version of their lives as their 'reality', although they experience and manifest contradictory responses. Thus many women come to believe that child care and home-making are their destiny, or that despite intellect and competence, they are not suited for senior management. This does not mean they are content with these beliefs, but probably that they accept their distress as a personal failure rather than a power issue.

The interface between gender identity, sex roles and discrimination is additionally complicated. Gender is a crucial means of categorisation and social stratification in all societies (see Bleier, 1984); it is central to individual identity, life expectations and opportunities (Rohrbaugh, 1981); and sex-role stereotypes in western societies reflect what women and men do, while at the same time serve as the basis for inequalities and social sanction. As Glynis Breakwell (quoted above at the beginning of this chapter) asserts, it is difficult for women and men to step too far beyond stereotypical behaviours without dire consequences. Women who achieve professional success have made an important step beyond the bounds of conventional femininity and women's role requirements. How do women senior managers cope with junior male colleagues who subvert their operations just because they object to a female boss? How do business women negotiate sufficient reward for themselves when work-related lunches and exclusive club membership feels alienating and stressful rather than a 'bonding' experience?

## Becoming gendered

Life span development and career are related concepts. Career progress and the context of a person's life are clearly and unequivocally linked to her family and the broader social context (see Chapter 4), as well as her sense of identity and personal integrity. Studies of life span development that tend to focus upon male development position women primarily in the context of their nurturing role in the family (Erikson, 1968; Levinson, 1986) and thus have little to offer to the theorisation of women's professional achievement.

The overwhelming fact about adult psychological development is that it involves *accumulation of experience*, and that experience is crucial to the way individuals act (see Chapter 2). Studies of child cognitive (e.g. Kohlberg, 1966) and social and behavioural development (Mowrer, 1950) have shown that gender is salient to the way children and adolescents adapt their cognitive and behavioural strategies. Psychological development and socialisation in the family, school and wider social context, guarantees that these strategies are incorporated into an individual's repertoire of knowledge and behaviour, which is a major source of gender differences in behaviour and temperament (e.g. Gilligan, 1982; Bem, 1974).

The consequence for professional women of socialisation and development in a specific context is likely to mean that aspects of their beliefs about gender become increasingly difficult to sustain. They are no longer fitting the expected gender life span path, and their chosen route is less clear for them than for their male colleagues. However, despite socialisation and development through common life stages, each person has their specific means of being themselves.

Studies of gender issues in school, higher education and training provide data on differences in intellectual, social and personality aspects of performance and behaviour at various points of the life-course. Research on behavioural differences at school between boys and girls shows girls working more consistently at academic work, although very few distinctions in personality or intellectual ability have been demonstrated irrefutably (Maccoby and Jacklin, 1974).

There is, however, evidence that teachers' expectations and behaviour towards boys and girls differs, and working-class girls in particular are expected, and consequently expect, to be primarily mothers who may work to subsidise the family income (Beckett, 1986). There is also some data to suggest that girls and young women feel they are less intellectually able than boys and young men (Beloff, 1992), and believe that menstruation disadvantages them in terms of exam and other cognitive performance (Richardson, 1992; Walker, 1995), although there is little conclusive evidence that this is so.

## Sex-role stereotyping

> Girls in our society are socialised to be more oriented towards people, to be other-directed and dependent, whereas boys are raised to be more independent, aggressive and achievement-oriented. Girls develop a negative self-image when they accept society's more positive evaluation of males particularly to succeed at 'work' is to demonstrate masculine traits, something most women are reluctant to do.
>
> (DeLameter and Fidell, 1971: 7)

Sex-role stereotyping is pervasive. Scientists, social opinion leaders and everyday beliefs reinforce traditional views of women's and men's characteristics, and these beliefs make a crucial contribution to organisational structures. Broverman et al.'s (1970) small-scale but influential study demonstrated the view that health professionals have about the 'mentally healthy adult' and social desirability for women's behaviour. Women, if they are to be feminine, are unassertive, interested in their appearance, dependent, illogical and focused on home and the family. While this equated with images of femininity, it is not representative of the successful career person. Subsequent studies of sex roles have shown that while these characteristics cluster together as a gross stereotype, they cannot be dismissed as they represent much of what women actually do and expect in their lives. Girls are socialised actively into being feminine (Beckett, 1986) and the experience of psychological development involves girls in recognising what girls do, and thus beginning to identify their own thoughts and behaviours with this (Kohlberg, 1966; Bem, 1981; Hargreaves, 1986).

Classical psychoanalytic theory, which has had a greater influence on popular culture than on academic psychology itself, also suggests that normal and healthy femininity equates with passivity. 'Normal' women are passive and responsive to men in their actions, personality, sexuality and other relationships, and Freud himself was clear that women who achieve in careers may suffer from 'penis envy' (Freud, 1931a), which will have long-term negative psychic consequences.

> The little girl, frightened by the comparison with boys, grows dissatisfied with her clitoris, and gives up her phallic activity and with it her sexuality in general as well as a good part of her masculinity in other fields. The second line leads her to cling with defiant self-assertiveness to her threatened masculinity. To an incredibly late age she clings to the hope of getting a penis some time. That hope becomes her life's aim; and the phantasy of being a man in spite of everything often persists as a formative factor over long periods.
>
> (Freud, 1931b, quoted in Bocock, 1983: 53)

Freud and followers of his theory and practice claim power, influence and assertiveness in the public sphere as 'naturally' the province of men. They argue that women 'naturally' gain their greatest satisfaction from giving birth and motherhood – particularly if they should have a boy. These issues are explored more fully in chapters 3 and 4, when considering the interface between gender identity, beliefs and experience.

## SUBJECTIVITY

How does the gendered person negotiate their psychological development and social interaction? How do women and men make sense of their gender in the world of work? Psychologists traditionally have talked about personality, intelligence and situational variables as influencing behaviour and experience in organisations, and make claims to select suitable candidates for management positions through the use of psychometric tests and standardised interviews (Alimo-Metcalfe, 1994). This process relies on the assumption that the person/individual is somehow an objective, measurable and observable object.

As Sampson (1989) demonstrates, despite 'six discernible challenges' from a variety of different epistemological directions, North American (and thus British) mainstream psychology has adhered stubbornly to the validity of the unitary individual whose personality, behaviour and cognitive abilities might be objectively measured.

Feminist, and critical social psychologists in particular, have challenged the fixed notion of the unitary individual. 'This concept describes a fictitious character, the bourgeois individual, whose integrated wholeness, unique individuality and status as a subject with actual power to shape events has become null and void' (Sampson, 1989: 3). Instead of concepts such as 'personality' or 'self', critical writers have focused upon the dynamic interaction and fluid boundaries between the social and the individual, and have identified *language* as the means by which interaction takes place (Potter and Wetherell, 1987). Language and social discourse produce the means by which the social and the individual interconnect and disconnect, and these processes occur over time and during the course of specific actions (see Chapter 2).

In the context of this book, I wish to demonstrate the complex and contradictory ways in which a sense of being a gendered individual in a male-dominated culture and organisation influences the ways in which integrity and survival are negotiated. Women's traditional roles and responsibilities in relation to men (at home and at work) are integral to the experience of being a woman. Gender discrimination, subordination at work and the experience of being socially and professionally marginalised further influence everyday experience and become integrated into a sense of subjectivity/identity. Resistance to patriarchal processes occur as women refuse to accept the pre-existing categories and roles, while at the same time, as argued earlier in this chapter, women's lives are circumscribed by gender role expectations. Femininity is a contradictory experience, and as such individual identity or subjectivity is experienced as a connection/dislocation between the social and the subjective.

As Harré and colleagues suggest:

> a human mind does not emerge out of processes internal to the human individual. It is a shaping of the activities of the whole person, including their brain and nervous system, by sociolinguistic influences. In the course of this shaping a person acquires a fragment of the rules and conventions of their society, in accordance with which they form projects for action and choose the means for realising those projects.
>
> (Harré et al., 1985: viii)

Deconstruction and discourse analysis, as a method in social science and psychology in particular, has demanded detailed scrutiny of the concepts of 'self', 'identity' and 'subjectivity'. The terms 'self' and 'identity' have traditionally been associated with mainstream notions of the unitary individual, and while some post-modern, deconstructionist social scientists would stress that there is nothing *but* text (see Sampson, 1989 for discussion, and see also Chapter 3), I argue here for the preservation of the project of a reflexive self/identity/subjectivity (see Giddens, 1993) and biographical accounting (see Chapter 2).

What is important is to stress the fluidity of the boundary between subjective experience and the social world (see Chapter 7), and particularly the relationship between gender as a social process and gendered experience (see Tunaley, 1995). Thus there is no essential biologically determined female experience, but being a woman, including the capacity and reality of child bearing, is a socially constructed and dynamic process (see Chapter 3).

## WHY FEMINISM?

> modern science conceives itself as a search for knowledge free of moral, political, and social values.
>
> (Riger, 1992: 730)

> The theme of women's biological inferiority has been both implicit and explicit in biological science since the time of Aristotle. It is ... an essential theme for the ideology and cultural practices of society that require women's subordinance both in the home, as homemakers and mothers, and in the marketplace, as underpaid workers in the nurturing, helping and domestic professions.
>
> (Bleier, 1984: vii)

All knowledge – popular, scientific and professional – is male dominated. This includes the knowledge underlying scientific and popular beliefs about women which are held by women and men and acted on in some way by everyone. Feminist science, particularly that emerging from psychology, biology and social science (the traditionally accepted knowledge bases which claim to explain human behaviour and experience) has continued to challenge dominant models of research and theory while building up feminist models of human experience and behaviour. In developing a feminist psychological perspective on gender, power and organisation, the experience of women as academics and scientists is especially relevant for exemplifying some of the crucial issues.

Feminist scholars have been consistently concerned with challenging the stated aims, objectives and methods of positivist science (Harding, 1986) and the developing critiques have gained momentum and influence, particularly since the early 1970s (see Henwood and Pidgeon, 1995). The emphasis of these critiques, encapsulated in the quotations above, is twofold.

The first is the traditional scientific insistence on 'context stripping' as a function of its preferred methodology, and the consequent failure to take account of the implications of this for the construction of knowledge about women. The second is the identification of the clear sense in which positivist science, far from being value-free, exhibits a demonstrable bias towards the 'pathologisation' of women, particularly in relation to reproductive and mental health (Ehrenreich and English, 1979; Bleier, 1984; Ussher, 1993).

Psychological science traditionally has followed the path of the natural sciences, both conceptually and methodologically, and as a result accorded little credibility to the claims of feminist scholars and researchers. Those who argue that the discipline has marginalised and pathologised female experience are themselves marginalised from the mainstream of psychology (Sherif, 1987; Ussher, 1992a). Psychology has failed to recognise the implications of that process of exclusion for the way that claims to psychological knowledge are constructed (Sherif, 1987). This has not been so much the case with other social science or humanities disciplines, where the influence of critical theory and postmodernism have enabled sympathetic scholars to engage in epistemological debates taking account of feminist perspectives (Campbell, 1992; Riger, 1992).

## Methodological and conceptual issues

The orthodox answer to the question 'How did psychology come to be what it is?' is that psychology is a science and, as such, is guaranteed through its methods, progress towards knowledge of that part of nature that it takes as its object. This begs a supplementary question, however, a question on the terrain of philosophy of science that would probably not be thought at issue in orthodox psychology: what is the character of that knowledge and how can we know that science guarantees its truthfulness?

(Hollway, 1989: 87)

Traditional academic experimental psychology employs reductionist methods which set out to *exclude* both social context and the structural/ power relations between individuals as inherent 'bias'. Of concern to feminists is that these methods and the consequent findings, by definition, fail to identify the relationship between certain kinds of behaviour and the consequences of patriarchy[1] and therefore reinforce what they identify as the 'natural' behaviours, for instance those revolving around gender stereotypical roles (Bernard, 1981; Crawford and Maracek, 1989; Nicolson, 1992c).

There is evidence that psychological science, by not problematising power and context, has actively contributed to the subordination of women through reinforcing misogynist mythology under the label 'science' (Nicolson, 1993a, 1995a). This is the case with studies of the menstrual cycle. Feminist psychologists have identified that women's abilities in a number of spheres have been deemed deficient behaviourally, cognitively and emotionally because of the conceptualisation of the research questions and associated methodologies (Parlee, 1990; Ussher,

1989). This work has been used to justify women's unsuitability for certain professional roles which claim to require an even temperament and sustained concentration; qualities that women, because of their 'raging hormones' are seen as lacking (Choi, 1994). However, careful re-analysis of data derived from these experiments (Sommer, 1992) and reassessment of the methods themselves in menstrual cycle research (Parlee, 1990; Ussher, 1989) have demonstrated the flawed nature of the evidence employed to legitimate female inferiority accorded by the fact of menstruation. Why, when there has been no shortage of criticism of the experimental method (e.g. Harré and Secord, 1972), does psychology avoid shifting from the experimental paradigm? Why, when feminist scholars have demonstrated the fallacy of claiming 'truth' about women through these methods, are psychologists so resistant to change?

Psychology makes its claim specifically to be a science *because* of its methods and its claims to ability to take a value-free stance towards its subject population. The goal of science – and thus psychological science – is through the 'objective' investigation of human behaviour, to make predictions and thus identify and construct laws, and therefore the 'truth', about human action (see Riger, 1992).

## Scientific knowledge claims, power and gender

Why specifically is the scientific method gender-biased? There are three problems with this adherence to the 'objective' investigation of behaviour for the way knowledge claims are made about women and gender differences.

> An experiment typically consists of a brief encounter among strangers in an unfamiliar setting, often under the eye of a psychologist. The question is whether this context is a valid one from which to make generalisations about behaviour.
>
> (Riger, 1992: 732)

First, as the experimental environment seeks to take the *behaviour* of the individual 'subject', rather than the 'subject' herself, as the unit of study, it becomes deliberately blind to the *meaning* of the behaviour including the social, personal and cultural context in which it is enacted (Reinhartz, 1985). Therefore its claims about gender differences in competence and behaviour are attributed to intrinsic rather than contextual qualities: they are either the unproblematic product of gender role socialisation, or are biologically based.

Second, experimental psychology, far from being context-free, takes place in a very specific context which characteristically disadvantages women (Eagley, 1987). Women under these circumstances, stripped of their social roles and accompanying power and knowledge (through a professional role or particular set of competencies through which she herself defines her capabilities), are placed in this 'strange' environment and expected to respond to the needs of (almost inevitably) a male experimenter. Here she will have lost any social power she has achieved in the outside world, and will be faced with the simple fact of her female subordinacy in a strange situation. Thus she will be an anonymous woman in interaction with a man who is in charge of the experiment, with all the social meaning ascribed to gender–power relations (Leonard, 1984).

Third, and perhaps most crucially, scientists fail to take account of the influence of the relationship of power to knowledge (e.g. Foucault, 1978). The way that knowledge claims about women's psychology are structured, and the power of dominant social groupings employing vested interests to set norms and influence popular knowledge, are also crucial to understanding the genesis of research paradigms and human socialisation. The priority western society attributes to science is more problematic in the late twentieth century than ever before because of the relationship of science to the media which influences human socialisation. Psychology relies for its data on the practices of socialised and culture-bound individuals, so that to explore 'natural' or 'culture-free' behaviour (i.e. that behaviour unfettered by culture, social structures and power relations) is by definition impossible, which is a state of affairs that normally goes unacknowledged.

The interconnectedness of science, the media and the gendered self-concept/identity/subjectivity therefore needs to be explored when assessing the validity and legitimacy of scientific knowledge claims. The press and broadcast media report scientific 'discoveries'. Individuals become so familiar with these, that they are influenced in the way they assess their own behaviours in relation to the scientific 'norms'. They respond in ways that link their own sense of being to these and when these individuals themselves are the subjects of psychological research their relationship to the norms created by scientists are revealed in the findings and lend support to the original claims (see Nicolson, 1993a for further discussion of this argument).

The status of the contribution of the experiment to psychological knowledge, then, has been challenged because of limitations imposed on the discipline by those same methods and theories that inform them (Harré and Secord, 1972) and through the relativist challenge to the idea of 'truth' (Shotter, 1993). Thus, rather than seeking the 'truth' to a research problem, the central theme is: the world of human existence does not exist independently of human activity, but is a product of that activity – in particular that world is constructed discursively (Harré, 1993: vii).

The challenge from a post-modernist perspective has been increasingly effective in social and biological science, arguing that 'science as knowledge is fabricated rather than discovered' (Fox, 1993: 16); a perspective which is increasingly present at the periphery of social psychology and gaining a robust presence within feminist psychology.

It is from this relativist rather than a typically realist position that the contribution of psychology towards the subordination of women may be problematised. Traditional psychology, which fails to take account of the complex relationship of the human subject population and popular culture, is itself constructed via the discursive relationship between science and belief/mythology.

Traditional observation and measurement of behaviour leads psychologists to make claims about validity, truth and reality, ignoring the pervasive belief systems about gender relations through which both popular knowledge and scientific ideas are constructed and reproduced (see Nicolson, 1993a; Fox, 1993).

## FEMINISM, GENDER AND THE PSYCHOLOGY OF WOMEN

This section explores the relationship between psychology and gender issues in the context of a belief system that legitimates and reinforces the apparent neutrality of academic psychology and gendered subjectivity. The context will be explanations of gendered behaviour in professional and organisational life and how this influences popular knowledge of women.

### What is feminism?

The issues that have concerned feminist scholars within social science over the past twenty years, identified above, have been well rehearsed (see Wilkinson, 1986; Henwood and Pidgeon, 1995; Griffin, 1995). These include identification of sexist attitudes underpinning research questions exacerbated by the traditional scientific method (Condor, 1991) and the pathologisation of women in scientific knowledge claims (Ussher, 1989). However, the notion of feminism, with the various meanings attributed to the term, have meant that it is a complex and problematic concept.

A recently offered definition that 'Feminism is, especially, but not only, about women, but it is primarily the activity of giving them a voice, an access to power hitherto denied' (Thom, 1992: 25) appears to capture the spirit of both academic and political pursuits. However, this apparently simple statement reveals multiple layers of complexity and contradiction. For many who identify themselves as feminists, women's access to power is achieved through action towards women's rights: achievements in terms of women's suffrage, legislation for rights within marriage and in relation to children and employment (Bouchier, 1983). Some feminists define themselves through their lifestyles, which may involve seeking social change through challenging patriarchal institutions, or living without immediate reference to men. For others, feminism involves the development of scholarly critiques of accepted values and knowledge (Campbell, 1992).

Thus within feminism itself there is evidence of many different voices, and it is far from a unitary or static concept:

> there is a naming of the parts: there are radical feminists, socialist feminists, Marxist feminists, lesbian separatists, women of colour, and so on, each group with its own carefully preserved sense of identity.
>
> (Delmar, 1986: 9)

Each of these groups define their path to women's emancipation through different perspectives on political action or scholarly pursuit. However, the majority of women do not identify themselves as feminists (Cockburn, 1993), which means that women's voices are likely to reveal contradictions in the definition and practice of feminism; raising more questions than answers about the role of a feminist psychology. This is certainly true for women in management and professional life who reject the feminist label (Kitch, 1994).

### Feminism and patriarchy

> feminism has been anathematised by men, in an attempt to put a stop to its appeal to women. The process has been effective. Many women who in their ideas and practices are demonstrably feminist feel obliged to hedge their views with, 'I'm not a feminist but . . .'.
>
> (Cockburn, 1993: 1)

Feminism is essentially a reaction to, and product of, patriarchal culture[2] and one of its significant roles has been to account for women's subordination (Stacey, 1993). But what is patriarchy? It appears to have had a variety of definitions, although it was originally used to describe the rule of fathers in the family. It is now more commonly used to describe the context and processes through which men, and male dominated institutions, including universities and other organisations that foster scientific endeavour, promote male supremacy. This can be through both control of access to hierarchical power or characteristics of knowledge claims.

One feature of patriarchal culture is the way in which feminism and the 'feminist' are positioned as unpopular (Davidson, 1988). The vilification of feminism and the women's movement has been achieved through universally derogatory images of 'the feminist' portrayed in the mass media. For example, the emergence of contemporary feminism was accompanied by the powerful and pervasive image of the 'bra burner',[3] a metaphorical woman who aggressively challenged the sexual appeal of the female body to men.

'Bra burning' became an international byword for women's liberation. Well into the 1970s, on both sides of the Atlantic, this remained the image which was most widely associated with feminism. So farcical did it seem that it put paid to any serious questions being asked (outside the movement) about *why* women wore bras, or why some women now chose to stop wearing them. Even the original connection with the Miss America protest was forgotten (Coote and Campbell, 1982: 12).

The imagery encompassed the idea that the feminist not only rejected her own desirability, but she also wanted to 'destroy' the female image, thereby depriving men of their pleasure and exhibiting an unsisterly 'envy' of more attractive women. This image was a media construction partially successful in its intent to remove serious scrutiny of patriarchy from popular culture. Instead of confronting the challenges feminism brings to patriarchal institutions, media attention focused upon *presentation of the feminist*, ignoring the substance of feminist scholarship. This remains the case so that:

> popular approaches to feminism often contain references to a style of dress, to looks, to ways of behaving to men and women, to what used to be called 'manners'. It is, in practice, impossible to discuss feminism without discussing the image of feminism and feminists.
>
> (Delmar, 1986: 7)

Most people's knowledge of feminist ideas are derived from such images. For most women, particularly senior professional women, to be a feminist is 'taboo' because of its apparent lack of appeal to the powerful male population (Kitch, 1994). This denial of feminism as an ideology of dissent or protest relating to the difficulties that ordinary women face in their daily lives, strengthens the view that only the unsuccessful, unattractive and bitter are inclined to feminism. The power of this (un)popular image of the feminist as unattractive, irrational and extreme has been effective in ensuring that the majority of women, even though they might harbour sympathetic thoughts, find the concept of 'feminism' and the identity of 'feminist' as repugnant. As with the discussion of the knowledge–power influence over socialisation above in this chapter, it is no accident that a report of one study of young working-class women was entitled 'I'm not a woman's libber but . . . ' (Griffin, 1989). Young women find their feelings and experience do not sit easily with the image of the feminist and they therefore distance themselves from it, although the study revealed many views that might be defined as feminist. The conundrum for the feminist scholar and researcher is therefore how to represent women's experience of subordination in the text or data without adding to their burden of misrepresentation.

If most women – and, in particular, ambitious, achieving women – do not see themselves as feminists, how appropriate is it to investigate their experience from a feminist standpoint? Despite its apparently unrepresentative nature, feminism is relevant to the progress and development of psychological science, primarily as it is concordant with the goal of conceptualising knowledge as a discursive practice, which takes social, cultural and individual aspects of behaviour, experience, thought and emotion into account. Feminism at the very least seeks to contextualise women's lives and explain the constraints, attributed by some to biology, within a social framework. It may be that through such endeavours women's beliefs about the way their lives should be may be emancipated from the constraints of patriarchal culture.

But how far is 'feminism' an appropriate form of academic pursuit? This raises questions for feminist psychologists about whether there should be a psychology of women, a psychology of gender or whether psychology is such that by its nature it is an inadequate host. These issues are part of a dynamic process through which the complex and contradictory levels of female experience and the discussion of an emancipatory but relative approach to psychology might be tackled (see Chapter 7).

## THE CONSTRUCTION OF FEMALE PSYCHOLOGY

Throughout its brief history, academic psychology has provided a clear message, implicit by default, on the psychology of women. It has:

> not only omitted the consideration of women and women's activities, it
> has also validated the view that those activities in which men engage

are the activities central to human life. It affirms that women are 'backstage' to the 'real' action.

(Crawford and Maracek, 1989: 149)

For example, motherhood and the domestic sphere of life are less visible in scientific research than the world of paid work, despite, or because, the majority of women spend a significant part of their lives involved in this domestic context. However, research on the world of paid work is about *men* at work. It is only through the endeavours of feminists that women's lives in management and the professions have been added, albeit marginally, to the research agenda (e.g. Marshall, 1984; Cockburn, 1993).

[ Psychology has further disadvantaged women by constructing a 'reality' of female psychology which is seen as of less value than that of men, actually consigning women to the home and child care, through evidence that their skills are more appropriate there, and that children need their mothers' constant and continued presence (Nicolson, 1993b). This presents a constant dilemma for many women (see Chapter 4). ]

It is not only the popular image of the feminist as identified in the mass media that devalues and discriminates against women. Images of women and female psychology underlying psychological and medical science emphasise the apparent *deficiencies* of the female body and mind (Nicolson, 1992b) and contribute to a distorted view of women's experience, which is presented as knowledge – as in the case of women after menopause who are portrayed as asexual, lacking in intellect, moody and physically unattractive (Gannon, 1994; Ussher, 1992b). As Linda Gannon demonstrated in her analysis of the literature of the characteristics of women after the menopause,

> The image of the post menopausal woman has taken two forms. The first is the grandmotherly matron, somewhat overweight, who occupies her time knitting and cooking; and the second is the irritable, depressed crone who occupies her time meddling in others' lives and gossiping. For both stereotypes, sexuality is conspicuously absent – the grandmother has fulfilled her sexual role in the form of maternity and no longer desires sex, nor do others find her sexually appealing. The crone has always been and continues to be sexually dissatisfied and unfulfilled – feelings compounded by the realisation that it is too late. Are these myths based on reality or derived from misogynist myths?
>
> (Gannon, 1994: 102)

This question is rarely asked, and even less frequently answered. The menopause and other aspects of feminine biology and psychology are portrayed from a masculine perspective, with women as disposable and lacking in human variety. Thus women are seen as less rational, less independent than men and their particular 'strengths' are qualities which lend support to the maintenance of the status quo in gender–power relations. Thus women in senior posts, likely to be reaching the age of menopause and beyond (in their mid-forties – the peak of their careers), are seen differently from their male peers. The latter are 'distinguished', 'experienced' and 'wise' while the former are marginalised for being asexual and irrational.

The role psychology has taken in research and the development of theory in connection with the vulnerability and deficiency of the female body and its influence on psychological processes is central to the way women are marginalised and pathologised under patriarchy (Nicolson, 1992a). For those psychologists who reject a feminist standpoint or whose claims to knowledge are not informed by feminism, women's behaviour may be observed and measured and is thus available to scientific laws.

For feminists, the psychology of women is problematic. Female psychology needs to be understood in a *dynamic relation* to the context in which academics typically observe and measure it. This means that scientific analysis of women's behaviour is only valid when contextualised within an analysis of gender–power relations. Without an understanding of the influence of patriarchy on female experience, subjectivity and behaviour, psychology pathologises women through identifying their lack of social power and the consequent 'naturalness' of their subordinate position (Hollway, 1989; Nicolson, 1993a).

Through the process of norm-setting, psychologists and other patriarchal scientists have constructed a world in which their own and popular expectations of behaviour and emotion are given credibility greater than those of the subjects of science (Foucault, 1973; Nicolson, 1993a). This situation has arisen because of the ethos within academic psychology. It is one in which its methods and objects of study are deemed to have transcended the need for questioning. There is an atmosphere which suggests the 'truth' has been identified and the continuing progress towards discovery, particularly in the case of 'female problems', such as menstrual difficulties, will be undermined if feminist critiques are permitted to enter the mainstream arena (Nicolson, 1992c).

Scientific resistance to feminist critiques of the pathologisation of women is supported not only by its own patriarchal establishment, but also by the popular appeal of science to women: if women are failing to achieve in the public sphere or are discontented with their domestic lot, then perhaps the blaming of the female body serves them well, and feminist concerns which raise the dual spectre of inevitable disadvantage co-existing with responsibility (either individual or collective) for change, does not. That women may want to see existing knowledge on the pre-menstrual syndrome or the influence of the menstrual cycle upon mood change as problematic, even though its existence by definition emphasises women's deficiencies, has been made clear consistently in feminist (see Laws, 1983) and non-feminist circles. Recent challenges from a feminist psychological perspective to the existence of post-menstrual syndrome (PMS), reported widely in the media, resulted in some psychologists receiving 'hate mail' from women who claimed they had fought hard to get their 'condition' taken seriously.[4] It is therefore not surprising that feminist researchers and theorists have anxieties about their own role in challenging patriarchal psychology with one potentially more concordant with evidence from research which takes account of women's subjective experiences.

## The psychology of women

The psychology of women is a problematic issue fraught with contra-dictions. Stereotypical images of women as nurturant, co-operative and passive are employed by some scientists as both inescapable justification for their traditional (subordinate) roles (e.g. Wilson, 1978) and as laudable qualities that would benefit the human race (e.g. Rossi, 1977). The work of Carol Gilligan (1982) illustrates this well. Her work on moral development focused on, first, the way that theory in this area was developed from empirical work with male samples only, and, second, her assertion that females and males have different moral orientations. She contested Lawrence Kohlberg's accepted view that the most sophisticated stage of moral reasoning was one that took account of abstract principles for justice, and argued that for women, moral choices are usually made within a specific context and concerned with specific individuals. The theme of her work is that women have a 'different voice' from men or the model of the 'normal' person described in psychology texts. Thus her work is a contribution to a psychology of women, but it is potentially dangerous in terms of concern with issues of equality as it neglects the relationship between power, science and the construction of knowledge; appearing to position women as essentially different from men. This feeds into the gendered model of women as less important than or deficient in relation to men, especially in a culture where abstract thought is valued over context-specific ones.

Women's behaviour and beliefs are constructed within a context in which powerful vested interests are active in constructing a version of female psychology that accentuates female deficiency or pathology. Thus a psychology of women is better understood as a dynamic product of gender–power relations – i.e. that the psychologies of women and men are actively structured in relation to each other (see Hollway, 1989). A psychology of women has to make sense not only of the limited domain of behaviour, but of the social context in which this behaviour is practised and produced.

## Feminists in psychology

There is an intrinsic link between the vested interests of the dominant group in relation to knowledge claims and practices (Foucault, 1973; Philp, 1985) illustrated by the powerful positions men have within academic institutions, which validate the methods and knowledge that are defined as psychology, and the characteristics of that knowledge (Nicolson, 1992c).

At present, within British university psychology departments the staff are mostly men (i.e. almost 80 per cent men, with 84 per cent of senior staff being men: Kagan and Lewis, 1990a), yet between 70 and 90 per cent of undergraduate students are women. Concerns currently being voiced are about the reduction in numbers of male undergraduates, not with the gender imbalance at the top of the hierarchy (Morris et al., 1990; Nicolson, 1992c).

Despite evidence of enduring resistance of individual women to gender bias in academic psychology (Sherif, 1987), it was only relatively recently that a coherent voice of feminism emerged in the USA and UK (Chetwynd and Hartnett, 1978; Burman, 1990a). Attempts to establish an audience within the psychological community led to the genesis of Division 35 of the American Psychological Association for the study of the psychology of women. It took another ten years for the British Psychological Society's Psychology of Women Section to establish itself, although in the mid-1990s there is evidence of widespread international groups of this kind officially embedded in psychological communities throughout the world (see Burns, 1990).

These initiatives have been accompanied by the formalisation and dissemination of feminist knowledge in journals (e.g. Psychology of Women Quarterly in the USA and Feminism and Psychology in the UK), regular newsletters, a growing number of books and some changes in the content of conferences, the composition of policy-making committees and among the community of postgraduate psychology students as well as some academics. However, the nature of patriarchy demands that such progress be met with a 'backlash' (Faludi, 1992).

While many women and some men in academic and professional psychology have responded positively to feminist developments in psychological theory and method, there is evidence that the powerful groups who control the discipline are prepared to offer strong resistance. Kagan and Lewis (1990a, b) have documented examples of verbal abuse, physical and emotional sexual harassment, open and unsubstantiated criticism of women's academic ability and evidence that even flexible child care arrangements can be circumvented by those in authority who wish to exclude women staff from certain activities (see Chapter 6).

The academic community has traditionally been conservative and resistant to the inclusion and promotion of women (Hansard Society Commission, 1990). In UK universities only 3 per cent of women are professors, 6 per cent senior lecturers, 14 per cent lecturers and 32 per cent contract research staff (AUT, 1990) with only 18 per cent of women occupying tenured academic posts in universities in the USA (Caplan, 1994). While there have been attempts on behalf on some professions (e.g. medicine and the legal professions, see Nicolson and Welsh, 1992; Nicolson, 1992c; and the police, see Anderson et al., 1993) to explore the reasons for women's apparent lack of success and to make concessions, there have been no similar initiatives in the academic profession. The control of knowledge is being preserved by the continued exclusion of women (Nicolson, 1994c).

## Feminists outside psychology

It is perhaps no surprise that some feminists who have trained as psychologists have rejected psychological knowledge and methods and even the title 'psychologist' because the theories and methods are inadequate for the intended projects (Hollway, 1989).

Others consider that the discipline has rejected their contribution:

> When I write as a feminist, I am defined out of the category 'psychologist'. When I speak of social structure, of power and politics, when I use language and concepts rooted in my understanding of oppression, I am told that what I say does not qualify as 'psychology'.
> (Kitzinger, 1990: 124)

Others, however, see an identity for feminists as 'anti-psychologists' as having a value in its own right (Squire, 1990). Squire argues that as 'anti-psychologists' it is important to develop a critical role towards psychology itself, rather than ignoring the role of psychology in the production of knowledge. This is not only of benefit to feminism, but potentially also for psychology, and is to be achieved by challenging psychological knowledge on gender issues by presenting a strong and flexible critical repertoire and contributing knowledge from other disciplines to psychology. This is something that rarely occurs because psychology is traditionally 'jealous' of its boundaries.

However, for the majority of feminists trained in psychology, the temptation remains to identify as psychologists, claim their rights towards the production of psychological knowledge while attempting to redress the claims of patriarchy, and develop more appropriate methods and theory (Ussher, 1990a).

## The case for a feminist psychology

> a feminist perspective is important not just for feminist researchers, but for *all* research in social psychology[5]    and indeed social science more generally.
>
> (Wilkinson, 1986: 6)

Feminist ideas about psychology not only question the structure of the substantive knowledge base, but challenge the way in which psychological knowledge is understood, produced, ordered and privileged and the structures which identify and legitimise those who have the authority to make such claims. Feminist psychology also explores the potential for non-sexist and feminist research methods and theories.

While feminism has and continues to make valuable critical assertions about the character of psychological knowledge claims, it is important to examine the other side of the coin: the construction of feminist psychology itself. It is here that a valuable interdisciplinary framework has emerged.

Marxist and post-modernist sociology, social philosophy and literary criticism have all informed feminist ideas and have been incorporated into 'women's studies' (see Wilkinson, 1986; Robinson and Richardson, 1993). It is through these different approaches that feminist ideas about the subordination of women under patriarchy, the nature of ideology in human social practices (particularly science) and the relative nature of knowledge, were made explicit. It is from these roots that feminist ideas emerged in psychology, although not without criticism. As Burman (1990b) has argued, while post-modern ideas provide insight into the construction of knowledge, they potentially confuse feminists about what form of action is appropriate for social change.

Male domination of the discipline, the recognition of sexism in knowledge claims (particularly in relation to cognitive abilities, socialisation and the way in which the female body was pathologised) and the development of feminist theory in sociology and women's studies in particular, comprised the springboard for the development of a feminist psychology (see Wilkinson, 1986). In the context of feminist consciousness and change in other disciplines, some psychology researchers challenged the framework in which they operated. Social psychology appeared to be a particularly fertile branch of the discipline as far as feminist ideas were concerned (Burns, 1990; Wilkinson, 1990). This is perhaps because of its peripheral position in relation to psychology, from which it provides critical commentary on the main body of the discipline and enables links with other disciplines, particularly sociology. Also, by its nature, social psychology is concerned with human interaction, and although the majority of social psychologists do not take a critical stance,[6] there is the potential within the framework of that speciality for attempting to explain social processes including power, content and discourse.

## CONCLUSIONS

Mainstream academic psychology focuses upon the individual as a unitary, integral, observable being whose behaviour can be measured to provide scientific evidence robust enough to make predictions. In so doing it ignores the interplay between the context and gender–power relations as part of that context. However, a psychological approach *per se* rather than a sociological/cultural one, is crucial for explaining and contextualising the *experience* of women in senior professional and managerial posts. This approach endorses the view that such women are *not* essentially different from other women and men, but that their desires and sense of selfhood are subjectively experienced and need to be understood discursively. To achieve this, a psychological perspective that is both critical of positivist orthodoxy and patriarchal supremacy is developed in this book.

## NOTES

1  There is a bias in traditional psychology which ignores the centrality of ethnicity, class, culture and sexuality also.
2  I prefer the term 'patriarchal culture' to patriarchy, which I employ to identify a set of pervasive values which privilege maleness/masculinity over femaleness/femininity, although not necessarily in a conscious or overtly misogynist way. It is simply the result of failure to challenge the assumptions underlying everyday experience and belief.

3  This represented one incident when, in 1968, feminists reacted to the Miss America pageant in Atlantic City by arguing that such displays of women degraded all women. To protest they put bras and girdles into a 'freedom trash bucket', and the flames were an addition from enthusiastic journalists (see Coote and Campbell, 1982).

4  The source of this information is confidential.

5  There is no reason why this should not apply to all sub-disciplines of psychology.

6  Social psychology on the whole is as much about measurement, 'objectivity' and experimentation as the mainstream.

# Chapter 2

# Gender, knowledge and career

## INTRODUCTION

⌈ A career for a man is like motherhood for a woman. Anyone who admits not
⌊ being completely enamoured with the role appropriate for his sex is
committing blasphemy.

(Prather, 1971: 20)

A professional career is still seen by many as unsuitable and unnatural for
a woman, although women are now accepted in professional roles. Thus
while a female barrister may be commonplace, her aspirations to become
a judge may be perceived as socially undesirable. ⌉

This chapter sets out the theoretical background to understanding
gendered subjectivity and the part it plays in the professional psychological development of ambitious and successful women. It examines the
ways in which gender and the experience of being a woman or man is
socially constructed, and the ways in which people interact within the
patriarchal context of the work organisation. Further, it explores what
women do in their lives and careers, to show how their sense of biography
and achievement develops from accumulated experience.

## CAREER AND PSYCHOLOGICAL DEVELOPMENT

The study of adulthood ... takes us beyond the focus on the self: it requires us to
examine the life course in its complexity, to take account of the external world
as well as the self, to study the engagement of the self in the world, and to move
beyond an encapsulated view of the self.

(Levinson, 1986: 11)

Traditional psychological theories of adult development are limited in
their scope and contribution to understanding career and achievement.
The sub-discipline of developmental psychology tends to focus on infant,
child and adolescent development, probably because cognitive and

behavioural milestones are more easily located *within* the unitary individual and tied to biology/body. Adult human psychology is complex and more difficult to disconnect from its social context.

Careers, for the adults focused upon here, are a crucial site of developmental potential and change. While the domestic spheres of life – especially relationships and the family – are important for early psychological growth, for professional women with career aspirations, the home and personal relationships are only one piece in the psychological jigsaw (see Chapter 4). Between the ages of about 18 to 60, adults develop skills and competencies in a range of tasks which are central to psychological growth. During this time of life professional women and men engage in their careers in ways that are different for each sex, for a variety of reasons. However,

> the normal model of career is one of continuous service and regular and steady promotion progress to positions of greater responsibility... careers which do not match such a model are thereby rendered 'imperfect'.
>
> (Evetts, 1994: 7)

This is unlikely to be the pattern for all but a few women – it describes the male career. Women may take career breaks or start late because of child bearing. They may start late because of lack of early expectations, motivation or advice.

## The successful woman

[To be successful in a career, a woman would have to negotiate her way around the dominant social expectations that accompany the female sex: principally that motherhood and its associated responsibilities should be paramount and other considerations subordinate (Rapoport and Rapoport, 1976). Careers to fulfil their potential for success have to be taken seriously, not only by the individual concerned, but by key people in the organisation. So what strategies have successful women developed to bypass prescriptions based on gender which consign the majority of women to junior levels in organisations?

Barbara White and colleagues (1992), in an attempt to construct a portrait of the successful career woman, found some obstacles in trying to be too definite. However, there were certain limited generalisations to be made. Among successful career women they found a predominance of first-born or only children. A significant minority had a tendency to have supportive parents who also encouraged a sense of autonomy, although the majority of their sample reported problematic relationships, especially with their mothers. However, this may have similarly led to a degree of autonomy in decision-making and tolerating frustration. Overall though, the group had parents who pushed them to succeed.

They tended to be middle class and had done well at school. Their personality showed a high degree of belief in their own abilities, and while acknowledging luck, they attributed their success on the whole to hard work. Successful women also had a high degree of self-efficacy, a high need for achievement and were seen to be more innovative than less successful women.

Many had had early career challenges which they successfully overcame, and while none had been involved in a formal mentoring scheme, all had identified an individual who had enhanced their careers. Women's motivation seemed similar to an equivalent group of men, and they gained a sense of pleasure and accomplishment from their successes at work. Those with children experienced conflict, and although women managed domestic issues in the family, they employed others to take on the tasks of housework, child care and so on. As White and colleagues conclude:

Many of our successful women mentioned the importance of persistence and stressed the need to 'keep battling' to achieve their objectives. They felt that success required making an extra effort and that the process of achieving success is harder for a woman to achieve, they also stressed that women should not allow their femininity to become an issue. Women were discouraged from having a 'chip on their shoulder' .... In addition, a number of our successful women emphasised the need to let those in power know their ambitions.

(White et al., 1992: 228)

This research suggests several potentially contradictory exemplars of the successful professional woman. She is single minded, tough, autonomous and finds a means of distancing herself from traditional trappings of femininity. This includes separation from the practicalities of domestic involvement, as well as rejecting notions of 'being' a woman. Successful women also recognise support and encouragement and continually make a case for their own advancement.

This 'portrait' is useful in a number of ways. It emphasises characteristics which are largely located in the individual – her personality and the way she is influenced by social context. However, there is little sense in which contradictory forces are conceptualised, particularly in the way these women negotiate their femininity, nor of the way the context and subjective experience interact.

As the researchers have shown, these women demonstrate certain behavioural characteristics which are directly comparable to those of men. But they are not men, which means the way they have accounted for themselves while participants in the study cannot be the end of the story. White and colleagues finish the book with quotes from women who say 'You have to decide what you want', 'Blow your own trumpet' and other calls for their successors not to undersell themselves, but also not to be like men. 'In summary, our successful group felt that women needed to be single minded, striving to meet their ambitions, persistent, professional, honest and, above all, to be themselves' (White et al., 1992: 229). But is it really possible for a woman to be a professional success without experiencing emotional costs?

## Socialisation and inequality

As a consequence of their belief systems, highly motivated and successful women, who have been socialised into an awareness of gender differences, are likely to see women overall as less able or motivated than men, while they themselves are the exception and equal to their male peers (Tajfel, 1978).

Young women entering professional life or university education with an ambition to reach the top are likely to have been encouraged and supported at home (particularly by their fathers: see, for example, Firth-Cozens, 1991) and at school, particularly if they have attended an all-girls' school (White et al., 1992).

In a series of interviews conducted for a study on gender inequalities in medical education (Nicolson and Welsh, 1992), women medical students, shortly after entry to their course, were indignant about suggestions of potential gender inequalities. They saw their achievements as equal to those of their male colleagues, and thus discussions of sexual harassment and gender discrimination represented to them an over-reaction or prejudice against men. Thus:

> There is no good reason to think that women and men are not seen as equal as they make equally good doctors.
>
> (Second year)

> A good doctor will be the one with the suited personality, therefore men and women can be equally bad and equally good.
>
> (Second year)

Several suggested that there might be good reasons for women to be excluded from one speciality or encouraged towards another. Thus some surgical specialities contain few women in senior posts because they may be:

> physically strenuous – such as orthopaedics, neurosurgery, cardiac surgery. There are physical differences between men and women.
>
> (Second year[1])

> For men surgery is more compatible with having a family, if a woman wants to have a family it is possible but nature and society are against her.
>
> (Fifth year)

Some young women argued that sexual harassment was something that sensible women could handle without fuss, and without help.

> Adults should be able to deal with sexual harassment themselves as they will not be protected forever. It's the victims who should report this to the University and get the culprits warned. If reports of incidents come from elsewhere there is a fair chance that they would have been exaggerated.
>
> (Second year)

They seemed unable to hear the 'bad news' that sexism exists, that universities and the medical profession are patriarchal and have deeply misogynist roots (Ehrenreich and English, 1979; Elston, 1993). However, these women's perspectives on gender inequalities change radically as the subsequent two or three years pass by (see chapters 4 and 5). They then learn to their cost that, like it or not, the medical profession like all others is a difficult place for women. They also learn that female nurses treat male doctors and even male medical students with more respect, or at least interest, than they treat female medical students and doctors. They also observe that male nurses prefer to deal with other men (Firth-Cozens, 1991).

Interviews with mature students[2] graduating in psychology from (what was then) a polytechnic, similarly demonstrated a previous naiveté about gender discrimination and the influence of gender roles and expectations on their lives. One woman, typical of many who had not seen career as central to her life said:

> I left school desperate to get married, so I'd done my 'A' levels and then run away from everyone's good advice and having got married and had my first child, I started doing an Open University degree which I got halfway through when my husband died and I had to go to work. I

really didn't think any more of it until my kids started doing 'A' levels and I thought either I'm going to spend my next two years washing up or we're all going to study together.

(Marshall and Nicolson, 1991: 27)

This woman's account gives an insight into the unconscious nature of the power of gender and the female role in determining key decisions, or the lack of them, connected with life and career. This extract is also engaging because it illustrates the importance of individual circumstances and biography for giving life its meaning, and as a unique position from which experience is understood.

So individual women and men have to grapple with their beliefs derived from the complexities of biology and socialisation, and adult psychological development, which impacts on and interacts with these. The framework employed here further challenges the notion of a static personality, or even the inevitable influence of social circumstances (see Introduction to Part I).

To theorise the individual as a changing and influential adult, it is important to unravel the complex psychological processes which produce and reproduce the social forces and consequences of gender–power relations.

## KNOWLEDGE, SELF-CONSCIOUSNESS AND GENDER

Women and men are subject to processes of socialisation or social influence throughout their lives. For those women in management and the professions, involved in large work organisations, these influences tend towards keeping them in roles of a status below their capacity and aspirations. This has a long-term negative influence both on those who submit and stay in the female 'role' and those who resist pressure to conform to gender expectations.

In order to survive psychologically, to step outside the bounds of ascribed gendered behaviours, to develop relevant capacities and skills and to affect social and political change, individuals need to achieve understanding and insight into their subjective experience. Women who are successful continually *negotiate* their psychological development in the course of their professional lives, and try to maintain their own sense of femininity/subjectivity in the context of gender–power struggles. Being a woman is undervalued in the professional context, which demands the ability to extend gendered strategies. However, femininity is also a compulsory requirement of being a woman (see Chapter 3).

To survive, a successful woman needs to confer meaning on her life, psychological development and career, which is based upon her own experience in the context of her personal biography and patriarchal power structures. How do we accomplish knowledge of ourselves in context in order to understand our own subjectivity, quality of our interactions and ascribe meaning to our lives?

Anthony Giddens (1984), a contemporary sociologist, offers a useful model as part of his theory of *structuration*. He argues that social scientists' focus of study should be 'neither the experience of the individual actor, nor the existence of any form of societal totality, but social practices ordered across space and time' (1984: 2). This perspective has resonance with critical social psychology and is particularly important here for understanding women's experience of *gender as a social practice*, involving women and men in interaction and in history, rather than a biological fact. Human action is defined by *knowledgeability*, which in turn requires *reflexivity*, which demands both self-consciousness and a sense of ongoing time. 'Human action occurs as a durée, a continuous flow of conduct, as does cognition. Purposive action is not composed of an aggregate or series of separate intentions, reasons and motives' (1984: 3). Thus the experience of being a woman entering a career changes and becomes part of the experience of subjective meaning. In other words a woman might say 'that was *my* experience, not that of a *woman*'. Thus meaning at any one time is, according to Giddens, a complex combination of dynamic change of *level of consciousness* in the context of time/life spans.

Giddens conceptualises human 'knowledgeability' as occurring on three levels – a 'stratification' model. These are the level of *practical consciousness, discursive consciousness* and the *unconscious*[3].

Practical consciousness refers to those things which the actor actually does. This is essentially implicit knowledge, to which the individual applies no scrutiny. Thus a woman might say 'I am assertive' or 'I always do badly at interviews' without thought or reflection, although it is something which the speaker/thinker recognises as characteristic at that time.

The discursive level of consciousness is the intellectual level at which knowledge is experienced. At this level, individuals reflect on what they know and do, and also experience the contextual and ideological element in this knowledge. Thus 'I am assertive' might contain the clue to a woman's contextual understanding of gender and patriarchy; it might be a means of consciously warding off competitors; or it might be a statement offered in order to receive a contradictory challenge.

There are no tight boundaries between the practical and discursive levels of consciousness, and socialisation through the course of professional life might modify the differences between the two.

The unconscious includes elements that are repressed from consciousness or are distorted. Giddens suggests that the unconscious incorporates a hierarchy of such material which expresses the 'depth' of the life history of the individual actor. As identified above, Freud and his followers believed that gendered desires and behaviours are a crucial part of the unconscious, and although Giddens did not accept this uncritically, the concept of the unconscious is important in understanding what binds an individual's life and part of the mechanisms/processes through which gender is expressed (see Chapter 3).

## CONSTRUCTING REALITY: CONTRADICTION AND TRUTH

When women, as in White et al.'s (1992) study, suggest that anyone can make it to the top so long as they are determined and play the game, they are making sense of their own experience to themselves as well as accounting to others. Each of us constructs and re-constructs our lives as a meaningful experience. We do this with reference to our understanding of the social context, and through positioning ourselves in relation to it. In other words, individuals constantly make sense of everyday reality in order to locate their position from which an understanding of both the past and future is drawn. This process has intrigued social scientists who reject positivist explanations of mental life.

> Everyday life presents itself as a reality interpreted by men [*sic*] and subjectivity meaningful to them as a coherent world.
>
> (Berger and Luckman, 1985: 13)

> when we talk about such entities as 'society', 'social relations', 'history', 'the individual', 'the self', 'persons', 'language', 'communication', – as well as 'ideology' – we can no longer assume that we know perfectly well what the 'it' is that is represented by the concept of the entity we are talking about.
>
> (Shotter, 1993: 37)

For traditional academic psychologists, there are 'facts' of everyday life – an objective reality. Some might even argue that biology, hormones and the desire and capacity to bear and breast feed children renders a career undesirable or even 'abnormal' (see Bleier, 1984). Many women and men believe this. Professional women who are also mothers may experience guilt and anxiety in their success because they are failing to be full-time mothers and failing to achieve as much as they might in the workplace.

Involvement in a patriarchal society and work organisation represents a different experience to each individual, and each negotiates their daily life in some relation to that. Expectations of everyday reality shape conduct, mark various points in individual lives, enable evaluation and negotiation of ourselves in relation to others (and others in relation to ourselves) and the social institutions through which we operate and are constrained.

The impact of gender stereotypes on experience and behaviour varies from individual to individual, throughout the life span. Despite the overwhelming evidence that women as a group are disadvantaged in professional life (see Introduction and chapters 3, 4 and 5 in particular), there are women who achieve greater success than most others, and who place gender in various positions of significance and power within their sense of everyday reality.

Some people will position gender as a more salient and influential aspect of their lives than will others, and as such it has a variety of manifestations. For example, for members of some cultures gender is explicit and central to women's lives. McLoughlin (1992) quotes from a female businesswoman and employer who says that Asian women see their own ambition as unwomanly:

> They think it is unfeminine to push themselves forward because in their culture women are subservient. In some of our offices Asian women did not want to be promoted to positions where they would be supervising men. The Asian men didn't want it either.
>
> (McLoughlin, 1992: 29)

In other cases gender becomes important when it is the source of struggle and conflict. Another woman in McLoughlin's sample of businesswomen said:

> Women will say it's actually bloody awful being the only woman in a group of twenty men – an experience I have continually – and it wears you down. They go to the pub and drink lots of beer (especially the British managers; the Europeans are a bit more sophisticated). When I started teaching here, I taught a course for a large British multi-national. On the first day I walked in and they said 'Hallo, darling, you teaching us today? What is a girl like you doing as a professor?
>
> (McLoughlin, 1992: 31)

Thus not only does gender become salient, but so does sexuality. This concurs with a recent discussion I had in Spain with a female interpreter with expertise in English, who told me that when interpreting for business*men*, she was expected, by her employers, to dress in a feminine and sexually attractive manner. This gave her clients the message that she was also available as a 'date' or even for sexual services. Although her contract hours and duties were clearly laid down, the fact of looking attractive as a woman inspired in men the assumption that she was sexually available. Her experiences led her to become more aware of feminist discourse, which she felt she would have ignored if she had not been exposed to this bad male behaviour that forced her to see her gender as critical in her working life. Her original vision of her work had been that her linguistic skills were the primary focus.

## Gender and the construction of success

Some women managers insist that their own lives and career success are independent of gender and that colleagues see them as a person rather than a woman (see Marshall, 1984). However, whether they accept it or not, women and men are gendered subjects in their work organisations or groups.

Some of the young female medical students quoted above in this chapter claimed that their career experiences were 'gender-free'. However, all these women are giving a meaning to the accumulated events in their lives. In these cases their sense of reality persuades them that their success has been on merit because they have been gender-blind. However, their early experiences may be perceived differently in retrospect, following later career struggles, the decreasing number of female colleagues as they rise up the hierarchy and, possibly, as they embark upon parenthood and domestic inequalities and potential conflicts arise from this.

Clearly there are traditional dimensions of inequality, such as social class and ethnicity, which distinguish between women. Even so, there are successful working-class and black women in the higher echelons of business, management and the professions. As a woman develops in adulthood, with the immediate experience of professional qualification, the development of competency and success, she interprets her world in a dynamic multi-dimensional way. This interpretation and consequent set of actions are both a response to and help to shape her reality.

In the following extract from an newspaper interview with a successful barrister, Nadine Radford (subsequently a QC), the complexity of gender in biographical accounting may be seen:

She ... was called to the Bar in 1974. At that stage there were very few
women barristers who were actually married. 'Women were routinely
asked about their plans to have children. I remember when it was
considered a breakthrough to have *one* woman in every Chambers.' In
her own Chambers she is now one of 9 women (out of 38 people)
although she is clear that she does not want to be seen primarily as a
representative of her sex. She recalls with affection a new clerk
referring to her as 'sir', typical of how he would address her male
colleagues. To Nadine Radford this was acceptance.

She believes that to succeed as barristers women need to break free
of the stereotypical notion that they need concessions, and should
expect to be judged according to their ability as barristers. Women
also need to be seen as having expertise beyond that involved in
sexual abuse or rape cases, Radford argues, where they are easily
sidelined.

(Nicolson, 1995b: 31)

She identified herself firmly as a woman, but saw the title 'sir' as
acceptance in a gender-free, rather than sexist, world. It was also pertinent
to the tale that she had to justify her motherhood arrangements in a way
that no man would have to. However, her experience was contradictory in
that in spite of being a woman – and possibly being marginalised – she
negotiated a sense of reality which enabled her to find a means of
achieving. Another successful young woman lawyer, Geraldine McCool
said she:

feels personally sheltered from being sex-stereotyped or discriminated
against. 'This does not mean that I am unaware of battles still being
fought in some firms. The problem is massive, particularly for women
with children. I've seen time and again how women are forced to
change their priorities when they have children. They put their families
first, and male colleagues moan'. She firmly believes that these female
solicitors make an emotional decision that they will continue to work
well, but the cost for them is that they give up ambition.

(Nicolson, 1995c: 30)

These two different versions of the reality of gender experienced by
successful women involve them in positioning themselves beyond the
reach of effective discrimination, but in different ways. Radford, a
barrister in a traditional Chambers, mother of three and in her mid-
forties, suggests that gender structures might be rendered insignificant
provided the woman in question is able to see them for what they are and

carry on regardless. She proposes the importance of avoiding stereotypical 'women's work'.

McCool, on the other hand, notably young, in her early thirties without children, and in a new and innovative area of the law, cites luck and not being a parent as contributing to her ability to negotiate hierarchies. She compares herself to other women who have children, and although she is sympathetic to them, she also positions them (albeit through no fault of their own) as being less career oriented.

She also recognises the ways in which stereotypical feminine qualities, such as interpersonal skills, have assisted her to develop strategies for surviving in her work.

> McCool thinks women rather than men, find interpersonal skills of that kind easier to acquire. 'Women recognise that the work is emotional as well as legal. I myself have something of both to offer clients'. She suggests this as a reason she has not experienced sexist attitudes from clients, in contrast to colleagues on the corporate side of the personal injuries equation who frequently have different stories to tell.
>
> (Nicolson 1995c: 30)

Both women take women's rights to equal opportunities seriously, both are outstanding in their careers, and both position themselves as different from other women but still able to utilise their femininity. The *fact* of their difference from other women is crucial.

Vicki Bruce, whom I interviewed for *The Psychologist*[4] (June 1991), at the time held a Chair in psychology at Nottingham University. Only relatively few women hold such positions, and as with other successful women, she demonstrates a capacity for distancing herself from gender issues. This is done here by distinguishing gender as a political issue separate from being a woman and being sympathetic to individual women. Bruce's work on computer modelling of the human face encompasses the field of human perception and face recognition and does not address gender issues at all, other than in terms of gender differences in research design.

> 'I do despair that I don't attract more women to work with me. I get women doing my options if they are called "face perception", but not if they are called "computational vision". I would love to do anything I could to get other women interested in the subject I am interested in . . . .' In her career she is not convinced that gender has been an issue as she has almost always worked in the predominantly male organised system.
>
> 'Being a woman has not been up-most in my mind – although if you

are in a minority, you are distinctive. It can work both in your favour
and against you. There are still people who find it hard to deal with
women at any stage of their career.'

(Nicolson, 1991b: 261–262)

She has positioned her own experiences of gender as incidental to the
arena of knowledge, power and work – a strategy adopted by many
successful women.

By contrast, Sandra Bem, Professor of Psychology and Women's
Studies at Cornell University, interviewed for the same journal by Celia
Kitzinger (May 1992) declares herself to be a feminist psychologist. She
talks of the discipline of psychology as bolstering male power, and
recognised the centrality of gender politics in her own life.

It dawned on me to try to integrate my personal and political interests
with my professional interests. And so I decided to start over and define
gender as my research area, and to do research and develop theory in
the service of my personal and political goals as a feminist. My research
interest has always been frankly political, and my major purpose a
feminist one.

(Kitzinger, 1992: 223)

Bem's early psychological work that gained her her reputation was the
development of the Bem Sex Role Inventory. Although her theoretical
perspective challenged social divisions into stereotypical masculinity and
femininity, neither her central argument nor her methodology were
revolutionary. However, in her interview with Celia Kitzinger she made it
clear that she has now taken a more radical standpoint on gender and
psychological research. She has faced the issue of gender inequality in
psychology and academia head on, and in her recent book, *The Lenses of
Gender* (1993), she declares: 'I have been writing this book in my mind for
over twenty years' (Bem, 1993: xi). She considers that it is more
acceptable to present as a feminist psychologist in the mid-1990s than
in the 1970s.

## BIOGRAPHY

Psychological experience and the development of a subjectively meaningful account of career progression is cumulative. Sandra Bem reported
the evolution of her ideas as emerging from her undergraduate days and
the development of her relationship with her husband.

When Daryl and I started to think about getting married, I began to realise what it meant to be a wife, and it didn't seem to me to make any sense. I wasn't going to darn my husband's socks, or wash his floors, or follow him around the country for his work. I wasn't prepared to sacrifice my life for his. So we stayed up the whole of one night talking, and we decided we'll just leave the kitchen floor dirty, and when it feels like we can't stand it anymore, then we'll wash it together. And we'll buy so many pairs of underwear, so that the laundry doesn't need doing very often, but when it does we'll do it together.

> (Kitzinger, 1992: 223)

It is not clear whether they achieved this, although their mutual career success probably resulted in their being able to pay someone to take on the housekeeping tasks. What is interesting is the dawn of feminist consciousness and its influence on career in the case of Sandra Bem in contrast to most other successful women, for whom a feminist label is perceived as an impediment.

As each woman progresses with her life and career, experiences at each stage have subjective meaning, and the meaning itself will have been interpreted and incorporated into the individual's accumulated *biography*; that is 'The common sense view. . . that we live through a certain sequence of events, some more and some less important, the sum of which is our biography' (Berger, 1966: 68). Thus the successful manager, who knows what she wants, makes it clear to her seniors and 'blows her own trumpet'; she will interpret her success as a result of these kinds of qualities and strategies. Bem has perhaps chosen to interpret her success as putting her life story into her research thesis. Other women might interpret their career success as the result of luck, ability, the situation or suitable mentoring.

Biography is experienced and understood within a prescribed social context, thus:

> The socially constructed world must be continually mediated to and actualised by the individual, so that it can become and remain indeed *his*[5] world as well. The individual is given by his society certain decisive cornerstones for his everyday experience and conduct. Most importantly, the individual is supplied with specific sets of typifications and criteria for relevance, pre-defined for him by the society and made available to him for the ordering of his everyday life. This ordering. . . is biographically cumulative. It begins to be formed in the individual from the earliest stages of socialisation on, and then keeps on being enlarged and modified by himself throughout his biography.

> (Berger and Kellner, 1964: 303, original emphasis)

The notion of 'biography' therefore enables theorists and researchers to take account of current and retrospective considerations in the way people account for their lives, while individuals give meaning to their lives within a socially prescribed framework which takes account of social organisation and structure including gender.

Underlying the use of biography as a conceptual framework and methodological technique is the view that the individual, others in her life and the researcher may have different ideas about what is important and what is not, and these judgements are invariably made retrospectively.

Biography, then, provides a practical framework for understanding how accumulated experience may be interpreted and reinterpreted by the woman herself, and thus giving an opportunity to understand the perspective of those who interact with her, or for whom she is a research subject or object of scrutiny.

## REFLEXIVITY

It is by means of reflexiveness – the turning back of the experience of the individual upon himself – that the whole social process is thus brought into the experience of the individuals involved in it; it is by such means, which enable the individual to take the attitude of the other toward himself, that the individual is able consciously to adjust himself to that process, and to modify the resultant of that process in any given social act in terms of his adjustment to it. Reflexiveness, then, is the essential condition, within the social process, for the development of mind.

(Mead, 1934: 134)

How does an individual make sense of and monitor and account for her biography? What psychological processes is she able to draw upon to place experiences in context and give them meaning? An important psychological mechanism, crucial to making sense of experience is the process of *reflexivity*. This concept was introduced above in the discussion of Giddens' notion of durée, through which individuals continually monitor their experiences. There are now a number of definitions of this which have emerged from recent initiatives in qualitative research in psychology (see Parker, 1993; Doherty, 1994; Nicolson 1995c). However, these are explicitly derived from, and intended to emphasise, the relationships between the research process, researchers and respondents. As Mead argued, it is also a constant part of daily life, and underlies subjectivity and experience and the way an individual constantly makes sense of her life.

## The 'I' and the 'Me'

Mead (1934) drew a distinction between consciousness and self-consciousness in human experience, which is useful for understanding internal 'conversation' and reflexivity. He was particularly interested in the way social interaction, and the internalisation of how we see significant others evaluating our behaviour and beliefs, influenced our self-conscious thoughts, and how those in turn were produced as a result of reflecting upon our consciousness. Thus:

> I talk to myself, and I remember what I said and perhaps the emotional content that went with it. The 'I' of this moment is present in the 'me' of the next moment. There again I cannot turn around quick enough to catch myself. 'I' becomes a 'me' in so far as I remember what I said. The 'I' can be given, however, this functional relationship. It is because of the 'I' that we say that we are never fully aware of what we are, that we surprise ourselves by our own action.
>
> (Mead, 1934: 174).

In other words in order to be reflexive, we need to see our self as the 'object' of thought (i.e. 'me') but the seeing is done by 'I', the subject. As Julie, in McLoughlin's study says:

> I don't enjoy chairing a meeting if it's on a contentious issue. If I've got to negotiate with the unions, and there's a situation of conflict, I find it hard to handle. I don't like doing it. I prefer a situation where things are informal, and that's not always possible. When I was at lower grades I saw taking decisions as exercising power, and I wanted to be in a position to take them myself, but I find where there's a balance of views I sometimes find decisions hard.
>
> (McLoughlin, 1992 : 87)

Julie is constantly monitoring her executive performance, and through the process of self-conscious reflexivity, she is able to position her developing self in a biographical context which enables her to continue observing her competencies.

In the following extract from an interview with Felicity (a respondent in a study of post natal depression: Nicolson 1988, 1995d) this process can be seen in detail.

PAULA: What made you decide to have a baby at this stage?
FELICITY: It's been a long process. A rather boring story.
PAULA: Not to me!
FELICITY: When we got married, Martin had had one by a previous

marriage. He didn't want to have any more children and I acknowledged this, and assumed we had come to some agreement. I didn't worry about it, but actually once we'd got married he decided he wanted children but I didn't know this. We understood one another on one level but not on another. Then we carried on quite a long dialogue – not really understanding each other. When I tried to think about it, it got harder and harder to make a decision. What happened I think is that I tried to take it all on myself, and I tried actually to work it out so that I could carry on working and in the end I just gave up. I couldn't think any more. I had put so much energy into thinking about it that I gave up.

(Interview 1: Nicolson, 1995e)

Felicity, through being asked to tell me about her decision to have a baby, actively engaged in evaluating her thoughts and behaviours both as she had done at the time and now, *retrospectively.* Evidence that this is what is going on in the interactive/reflexive process may be derived from the observation that I might find her ideas boring, through to her reflections on her relationship with Martin and his views on parenthood.

The reflexive process I am concerned with in the context of this book, however, involves the monitoring of experience and giving it meaning which is part of everyday life. The common feature between the quoted extract and the process of reflexivity is the *use of language in the action of explaining and contextualising self-action to one's self.* In the case of the research interview, reflexivity, as may be seen above, is stimulated by questions about the self as in certain kinds of conversations. However much reflexivity occurs in 'isolation', in which case language/conversation occurs 'inside the head', and it is this process that underlies the construction of biography and meaning of experience. This is only possible, however, because of previous access to conversations and gestures with significant others (see Mead, 1934).

## Supervision and reflexivity

In my role in relation to work supervision of senior professional women, I have observed the importance of reflexivity for the identification of the social context and, more importantly, *resistance* to patriarchal aspects of that context. The practice of taking time outside the immediate workplace to reflect upon the social processes may be empowering. It enables change and it enables recognition of the position of others in relation to self, rather than simply experiencing self through the eyes and behaviours of others.

I have argued in Chapter 1 and elsewhere (Nicolson, 1993a, 1994b) that the process of being a research participant in an interview study demands reflexivity, and thus potentially 'creates' a level of self-awareness through tapping the discursive level of consciousness. Thus, being a participant may be a therapeutic process. Further, the researcher is in a position to pick up and interpret non-verbal or unconscious verbal cues which may be fed back to the respondent for further self-conscious thought.

These processes occur in any focused interaction and are an essential part of counselling and therapy (Coyle, in press). The facilitation of reflexivity is valuable for enabling women to cope with the contradictory and stressful parts of their role. This is especially important for women in senior positions because they need to make sense of their *difference* from their male colleagues and other non-professional or junior women. This takes place while managing their identities/subjectivities as a woman in a man's world. The gender coping strategies employed by women managers (Marshall, 1984; White et al., 1992) invariably result in extra stress for women, even though (or especially because) they frequently deny the importance of their gender (see Davidson and Cooper, 1992).

In one example, Carole, a senior clinical psychologist who had been turned down for promotion twice, came to see me to see whether she could improve her interview skills, which she believed to be the main cause of her frustrations, as she knew she could cope well with the jobs she had applied for. Our discussion, however, moved quickly from her skills to focus upon the fact that some of her (predominantly) male colleagues made her feel inadequate. While she herself paid attention to the emotional aspects of social interactions at work, most of her male colleagues appeared to ignore, or even ride roughshod over, her emotional state. This made her feel less competent, as she perceived that she was being characterised in a negative 'feminine' way. When she attended promotion or appointment boards she believed that almost every other candidate was more worthy, and her not being appointed reinforced this.

It was through reflection upon her experience that she was able to talk about the way she felt about herself in relation to professional competence and subsequently reflect on herself in relation to others. This self-reflection led her to talk about her domestic life and identify how her husband, who worked part time in order to be more involved with the two pre-school-aged children, also made her feel inadequate in relation to his child-care skills. It turned out that while she saw her domestic responsibilities to extend beyond child care to domestic tasks such as shopping, cooking and bathing the children, his expectation was that she should do the latter because he was working with the children during the day.

Her own reflection drew her attention to her expectations, feelings and the way that her biography had developed to position her in her own eyes as incompetent because of the complex nature of the professional, emotional and domestic tasks that comprised her life. Thinking and contextualising in terms of gender–power relations at least gave her an awareness of the way men's strategies and expectations differed from her own, and thus she had the option to choose to set about changing her own, or choosing not to.

## CONCLUSIONS

In this chapter I have demonstrated the complex way in which gender is experienced. It is a key aspect of personal subjectivity/identity, and each of us positions ourselves in some relation to the traditional beliefs about gender/femininity. Through reflecting on our own biographies it may become possible to explain at least to ourselves how we came to be the women we have become. Many senior women, who feel that by being successful professionals they have turned their backs on traditional femininity, see themselves as different from other women. However, they do not lose an awareness of the fact that they themselves are women, and this provides an imperative to find an explanation about why they are different. The theoretical dimensions discussed above go some way to addressing those issues, while suggesting that despite the experience of distinction and success, at some juncture gender reimposes itself on all women.

## NOTES

1   The entry year to the course was Year Two.
2   Over 25 years at university entry.
3   Giddens acknowledges a direct relationship between this and Freud's psychic structures in the unconscious which contain the ego, super-ego and id (see Chapter 3).
4   The British Psychological Society's 'house' journal.
5   The term 'his' is in the original text.

# Chapter 3

# Femininity, masculinity and organisation

## INTRODUCTION

> What are 'masculinity' and 'femininity'? Every society has ways of distinguish-
> ing the sexes – socially, culturally, psychologically. Historically, however, the
> way this division has been drawn has varied enormously. What counts as
> maleness or femaleness in one period or cultural setting can look radically
> unlike its equivalents in other times or places. And similarly, how an individual
> comes to identify him or herself as belonging to a gender also varies greatly.
>
> (Maguire, 1995: 1)

> You cannot give the concepts of 'masculine' and 'feminine' *any* new connota-
> tion. The distinction is not a psychological one; when you say 'masculine', you
> usually mean 'active', and when you say 'feminine' you usually mean 'passive'.
>
> (Freud, 1973: 147–148)

From birth, we are compelled to seek confirmation of our gendered
identity. From the time we recognise whether we are female or male,
before we are sure we know how those in each category are meant to
behave, all human individuals actively pursue the project of 'becoming
gendered' (see Chapter 2). At the same time, we are aware of the
contradictions that separate experience and desire from social constraints
(Coward, 1993).

In this chapter I examine the multiple levels of meaning given to
masculinity and femininity and the significance for women and men in
their professional life. First, femininity and masculinity operate on the
level of the *biological/anatomical* body – hormones, genitals, secondary
sexual characteristics (Archer and Lloyd, 1982).

Second, at the level of the *gendered body* – what the shape, size and
appearance of the body means, particularly in terms of sexuality
(including desire and attraction/attractiveness), reproductive role-related
behaviours, the meaning attributed to hormonal/menstrual cycles
through the life span, and the way women and men use their bodies to

express themselves in a variety of interpersonal interactions (Choi and Nicolson, 1994).

Third, femininity and masculinity are associated individually and socially, with certain *traits/characteristics*, as in the Freud extract quoted above. Femininity means 'passive' and masculinity means 'active'. Sex role theories in psychology contribute to this by listing feminine, masculine and androgynous characteristics, and although female sex and femininity are not necessarily co-terminous, a woman whose main characteristics did not include feminine ones would probably be concerned, as there is an underlying popular belief system that women are like other women and men are like other men (Freud, 1973; Broverman, et al., 1970; Bem, 1987; Thomas, 1985, 1986).

Fourth, there is the level at which *gender–power relations* operate. Femininity and masculinity, women and men, co-exist in a constant power dynamic, which shifts its focus depending upon action or circumstances, but is nonetheless ever present (Bell and Newby, 1976; Leonard, 1984; Hollway, 1989).

Fifth, femininity and masculinity are contained at an *unconscious* level as a product of all these aspects of human experience and consciousness (Sayers, 1986, 1992; Frosh, 1994).

## ANATOMICAL AND BIOLOGICAL ASPECTS OF GENDER

> That women bear children and men do not is probably the most important biological difference between them.
>
> (Sayers, 1982: 7)

> The definition of women as weak, inferior and inherently unstable because of their dangerous sexuality and 'bleeding wombs' has long been the basis of society's and psychology's understanding of female adolescence, concealing reality behind the myth. It is during adolescence that the young woman first experiences a split between her body and her self: between her own experience and the archetype she is expected to emulate.
>
> (Ussher, 1989: 18)

It is difficult to separate anatomy and biology from their meaning, to either individuals or to society. The crucial aspects of anatomy and biology in relation to gender are the way that men and women are physically different, and that those differences are endowed with value which consistently disadvantages women.

Women's bodies, with the capacity for child bearing and breast feeding, are clearly different anatomically and biologically from men's. These anatomical and biological differences are the source of different behaviours associated with reproductive function. This is not in dispute.

What is problematic however, is the various ways in which the female body has been positioned as subordinate to that of the male (Ussher, 1989). This is often achieved in relation to women's reproductive capacities by patriarchal science operationalising female possibilities as if they were deficiencies. Thus, for instance, the menstrual cycle has been socially constructed by scientists, health professionals and the media as a disability. This myth has permeated popular knowledge. It is particularly important in professional life, because the belief that women are intellectually weak at certain 'times of the month' has been used implicitly and explicitly to count against women aspiring to senior roles. Who would want a barrister suffering from pre-menstrual tension to be their advocate? The idea of the surgeon or test pilot bursting into tears during the difficult part of the operation or flight is horrific. However, consistent evidence that only around 5–10 per cent (Warner and Walker, 1992) of the female population have menstrual disorders continues to be ignored in favour of these misogynist images. The same is true of the idea of cognitive impairment around the time of menstruation, even though it has been shown to be scientifically insupportable (Sommer, 1992).

However, not having menstrual periods is no safeguard for the image of the competent woman. Older post-menopausal women, who have brought up their children or who have simply taken longer to decide upon a career path, are also discriminated against for their lack of youth and femininity – the counterpart of their lack of fertility (Ussher, 1989; Gannon, 1994). As Jane Ussher says:

> The discourse which defines women through their reproductive function conceptualises the biological event of menopause as the end of a woman's useful life. As fertility and femininity are immutably linked here, women who lose their fertility often experience the simultaneous loss of their femininity a major part of their identity as a woman.
>
> (Ussher, 1989: 104)

Masculinity, on the other hand, is positioned as positive and competent in youth, middle age and old age. This is not to say that all men are destined to be successful in their professional lives; far from it. Masculinity is about competition, often to the 'death', with the rival. It is not uncommon for newly appointed senior managers openly to express hostility to rivals, particularly towards those in slightly junior positions who might be 'in waiting'. The male body is built to fight, and whereas the older woman is seen mainly in terms of her faded femininity, the older man, if he is no longer in the running for power, is seen as wise and experienced.

## THE MEANING OF THE BODY

Feminist social science, psychoanalysis and post-structuralist critiques have all made significant contributions to understanding the meaning of the gendered body, and feminists in particular to the power connotations of these meanings.

Here, I want to introduce the importance of the unconscious in the process of giving meaning to the gendered body, because of the relevance of unconscious processes to the way women and men interrelate in organisations and also the unconscious level at which organisations themselves operate. This will be discussed in more depth in Parts II and III of this book.

The meaning of the gendered body is a process rather than a set of facts, and this process takes place throughout an individual's psychological development, and responds to social development and change. The gendered body has a social meaning and personal/interpersonal meaning, following the framework set up in Chapter 2, it is difficult for an individual to experience one without the other. Thus we give our own body meaning which develops through our reflexive work in relation to different levels of consciousness, and this becomes embedded albeit in a dynamic way as part of our biography. However, the meaning we give our own body is bound up inextricably with the social construction of the female and male body. We evaluate ourselves accordingly.

### The body at work

As women demanded access to power, the power structure used the beauty myth materially to undermine women's advancement.

(Wolf, 1991: 20)

Women, valued by men and women alike according to cultural standards of 'beauty' are traditionally seen as valuable in relation to their reproductive capacity (Buss, 1994). According to Wolf, there is still no other way of judging women's worth, which presents a major dilemma for women who wish to be successful at work; being valued and valuing themselves at all stages of their career and life cycles. The 'beauty myth' discussed by Wolf represents an important cultural focus in relation to the female body. Women are valued by men for their beauty (associated with youth and reproductive capacity). Men have the economic power, which means that women need to compete with other women on beauty terms in order to achieve scarce male attention and ultimately to survive. As they get older, their value is less. This results in multi-million dollar industries aimed at sustaining and enhancing female beauty, who themselves have a vested interest in maintaining this beauty requirement.

All of these factors influence women's everyday experience in the workplace. Women have to be attractive, but if they are too sexually attractive they are dangerous and dismissed as mere objects of male desire, or both (Ussher, 1989; and see Chapter 6). If they rebel, and refuse to compete in the beauty game they are seen as ugly harridans.

The 1980s in Europe and the USA was the decade of 'power dressing'. Power dressing, or wearing business suits, might have been the 'answer' for aspiring professional women wishing to be attractive rather than sexy. Faludi (1992) discussing these repercussions associated with John Molloy's (1977) *The Woman's Dress for Success Book* said:

> for the next three years, women's magazines re-cycled scores of fashion stories that endorsed not only the suits but the ambitions they represented  with headlines like YOUR GET AHEAD WARDROBE, POWER! and WHAT TO WEAR WHEN YOU'RE DOING THE TALKING
>
> (Faludi, 1992: 210).

As both Faludi and Wolf point out, there was a fashion industry and media backlash against power dressing, although many women who did wear suits (a uniform similar to that of professional men) felt both comfortable and that it suited their behaviour and aspirations. Women were accused of looking masculine, although the kind of suits women wore were 'masculine only in so far as it established for women something recognisable as professional dress' (Wolf, 1990: 45).

Wearing more traditionally feminine clothes, particularly those that accentuate female characteristics (tight jumpers, short skirts) leave the woman in danger of provoking sexual harassment (Wolf, 1991; and see Chapter 6) and not being taken seriously as a professional.

As Wolf says:

> If, at work, women were under no more pressure to be decorative than are their well-groomed male peers in lawyer's pinstripe or banker's gabardine, the pleasure of the workplace might narrow; but so would a well-tilled field of discrimination . . . . Since women's working clothes – high heels, stockings, makeup, jewellery, not to mention hair, breasts, legs, and hips – have already been appropriated as pornographic

accessories, a judge can look at any younger woman and believe he is seeing a harassable trollop, just as he can look at any older woman and believe he is seeing a dismissible hag.

(Wolf, 1990: 45)

All women and men create and re-create their images throughout their careers. Undergraduates wearing jeans, with pink spiky hair, do not become academics, business women or lawyers without changing their image to a more conservative one. The emphasis as women and men enter the professional world is upon specifying their *difference*, although this in turn reproduces inequalities. It is clear what the professional man is expected to be, but the woman is left floundering with the strong possibility of falling into the trap that she does not look·the part.

But what is the significance of the difference between the ways in which the female and male bodies need to be represented? Despite understanding the politics and economics of gender and the implicit sexualised relations, there are important unconscious aspects of gender similarities and difference which provide symbolic meaning to the bodies of women and men.

## DIFFERENT BODIES, DIFFERENT MINDS

When you meet a human being, the first distinction you make is 'male or female?' and you are accustomed to make the distinction with unhesitating certainty.

(Freud, 1973: 146)

The differences between the male and female body are usually obvious, and this is accentuated through the way the individual is dressed and how they hold, move and generally control their physical presence. However, that the need for certainty in differentiating between the sexes is so important reveals the political importance of the gendered meanings given to the subjectivity of the person occupying the body.

Psychoanalysis, more than any other approach to psychology, links the body, mind, emotions and the social realms of sex and gender. Feminists, concerned with the way that femininity has been intrinsically linked with masculinity in a subordinate relationship, have turned to psychoanalysis to find a means to contest this intellectually and politically. Evidence achieved in this enterprise has served both to expose and implicate its proponents, particularly Freud, and to employ psychoanalysis to untangle the problem of subordination in the unconscious.

## Freud and femininity

Freud's work focused on the connections between human sexuality and its psychic development, and to explain this he describes the processes linking the body to the social realms and the achievement of masculinity and femininity and heterosexuality (see Freud, 1922). His method for achieving evidence consisted of his clinical case studies, and he extrapolated from these to develop his theoretical ideas.

Freud's explication of sex and gender was as follows. The human psyche has a tripartite structure: the *ego*, the *superego* and the *id* (see Freud, 1922). The infant is born with the id in place, which is the source of unconscious instincts and drives. During the first year of life the ego (or the self, the link with others and reality) begins to develop, and around the ages of 5 or 6 the super-ego, or conscience, begins to form. Although girls and boys are born with different genitals, they have no knowledge of this at first,[1] and thus there is little to distinguish their early psychic development. Their psychic development occurs through the journey of the libido through the body's erogenous zones: the mouth, the anus and the genitals. After the 'genital stage', during which the differences between girls and boys are ultimately recognised (around the ages of 5 or 6 there is a period of sexual latency which ends with the emphasis in adolescence on heterosexual genital sexuality. It is during the genital stage that Freud's ideas on femininity and masculinity are incisive.

Underlying psycho-sexual development is the infant's belief that everyone has a penis, and it is this belief and the discovery that not everyone does that brings about differential crises in girls and boys, which makes them identify with the same sex parent and separate themselves from the other. But because of these bodily differences, and the *value* of the penis, identification has different implications for both the psychic nature of each sex and the relations between the sexes. The one sex (male) *has* the desired penis while the other (female) *lacks* a penis.

Freud is clear that there is a path to normal womanhood and a path to normal manhood. These are achieved at the point where genital differences are noticed in the self and in the parents.[2] For the boy, who has unconscious sexual desires towards his mother, the recognition of the girl's lack makes him fear similar consequences, namely castration. To avoid the rivalry and wrath of his father the boy identifies with his father's masculinity, positioning himself with all men as different from women. This is the Oedipus complex.

Teresa Brennan (1992) summarises the Oedipus complex and its consequences as follows:

The boy resolves his Oedipus complex by anticipating the future: he will Have a woman like his mother one day; and this prospect enables him to defer the present unrealisable attachment in favour of a possible future goal. He defers at the same time as he 'smashes' his Oedipus complex by diverting the hostility originally directed towards his mother towards his father. Some of this hostility also finds its way into his sexual drive, which he splits off from his affectionate feelings towards his mother and represses .... The lynch-pin in the repression of the masculine Oedipus complex is the threat of castration. This threat, which can be a matter of reality but is usually phantasy, is what prompts the boy to repress his desire for his mother, identify with his father, establish a super-ego, and ideally redirect his drive into sublimation.

(Brennan, 1992: 12)

Freud was less decisive in his account of girls' resolution of their sense of lack, and it is the contradiction in his accounts of the development of femininity which is both intriguing and abhorrent to feminists (see Mitchell, 1974).

As Brennan summarises again:

Because this threat has less power in the feminine case, as the girl is already castrated, she has less motive for establishing a superego, and none for giving up her attachment to her mother. Indeed, the problem becomes why she should repress her phallic sexuality, as Freud of course maintains she does, and why she turns from her mother 'in hate', and forms an Oedipal attachment to her father.... Freud's main explanation for the girl's repression of her phallic sexuality and for her turning from mother to father is penis-envy.... She blames her mother for refusing to supply her with a penis, and turns instead to her father.

(Brennan, 1992: 12–13)

The girl's phantasy is that the father will supply her with a baby to substitute for the missing penis. Hence for Freud 'normal' femininity is enacted through childbirth and motherhood and other desires are neurotic, affirming the unresolved envy of the penis.

Freud's clinical work – and hence his case studies which provided the evidence for his theoretical stance – was almost exclusively with women. Thus, despite his persistent claim that he had theorised 'normal' masculinity and femininity, he was constantly faced with women who were not in accord with this norm. His response was to deem that they were 'neurotic'. In addition he consistently reiterated the idea that femininity was a 'riddle'.

> Throughout history people have knocked their heads against the riddle of the nature of femininity.... Nor will you have escaped worrying over this problem – those of you who are men; to those of you who are women this will not apply – you yourselves are the problem.
>
> (Freud, 1973: 146)

His view was that the male is naturally 'active' and the female 'passive' by virtue of their genitals and their function during sexual intercourse, which is only contradicted in women's 'active' behaviour in relation to caring for children (p. 148). Women have made no other contribution to society.

> It seems that women have made few contributions to the discoveries and inventions in the history of civilisation; there is, however, one technique which they may have invented – that of plaiting and weaving.
>
> (Freud, 1973: 167)

His evidence for the psychological importance of anatomical distinction in different characteristics in women and men is what he calls women's *castration complex*. When girls see the genitals of the other sex they consider themselves to be seriously wronged and 'fall victim to "envy for the penis", which will leave ineradicable traces on their development and the formation of their character' (Freud, 1973: 159). For Freud, these ineradicable traces may be seen in subsequent desire 'to carry on an intellectual profession' (ibid.: p. 159).

The seriousness of this lack is the turning point in a girl's development, and Freud argued that there were three potential pathways of development from that point: sexual inhibition or neurosis, change of character in the sense of a masculinity complex, and normal femininity (ibid.: p. 160).

Neurotic sexuality is to take on the 'active' role in relationships, which Freud argues comes from failure to abandon clitoral sexuality in favour of vaginal. This is only resolved 'if the wish for a penis is replaced by one for a baby' (p. 162).

The masculinity complex occurs when the girl continues to behave in an active way into adulthood, the extreme of which he sees as female homosexuality. Normal femininity is passivity and motherhood.

Of course, the issue is why Freud has these 'problems'. They are only problems for women as they represent the strains of patriarchal culture on freedom of choice and ability to achieve according to merit.

**Feminism and Freud**

Mitchell (1974) in *Psychoanalysis and Feminism*, argues that despite Freud's clear plea for the patriarchal status quo, through the judgement that women have to achieve femininity and may only do so through being wives and mothers, 'a rejection of psychoanalysis and of Freud's work is fatal for feminism' (Mitchell, 1974: xv). This is because Freud is not offering 'a recommendation *for* a patriarchal society, but an analysis *of* one. If we are interested in understanding and challenging the oppression of women, we cannot afford to neglect it' (Mitchell, 1974: xv).

She argues that Freud himself neither 'invented' the myths underlying the bourgeois family and patriarchal social structures, and neither did he unequivocally recommend their continuation. His thinking changed over the years, and he identified contradictions in his own work, as well as inspiring others such as Deutsch, Horney and Reich to take issue with traditional notions of female sexuality, passivity and 'women's place'.

Janet Sayers (1992) has reiterated Mitchell's point in relation to psychotherapy:

> It is no surprise to learn that feminists often reject this phallocentric account of women's psychology – at least for the first dawning of their heterosexual and maternal desire. So too do many psychoanalysts. Yet in doing so they have opted for psychological theories and therapies that assume and in the process overlook sexual difference and inequality.
>
> (Sayers, 1992: 196)

Nancy Chodorow (1994) has further stressed feminist abhorrence to the essentialism of Freud's psychoanalysis, but asks why the same critics remain intrigued by psychoanalysis, particularly its contribution to understanding gender divisions.

Certainly psychoanalysis and feminism are increasingly paired in the research and theoretical literature (Brennan, 1993), and there appears to be a consistent interest in Freud's work. However, recently post-Freudian psychoanalysis has taken centre stage, particularly in relation to under-standing sexual difference and accounting for female subordination.

## POST-STRUCTURALISM AND PSYCHOANALYSIS

> Femininity and masculinity are ways of experiencing the world. They are constructions which are built around anatomical difference, signifying only because they are given significance in the context of the power relations that constitute the social environment. Masculinity and femininity are subjective

positions, central to our concepts of self because we are constructed in a world divided along gendered lines, but in principle they are just positions, ways of seeing and speaking about what we see.

(Frosh, 1992: 154)

Through the work of post-structuralist psychoanalysts, following Jacques Lacan, it has been made possible to discuss this sense of gendered experience in relation to the physical body. Lacan, a psychoanalyst, was among the first to question the assumptions traditionally made about Freud's work. He was interested in understanding notions of the ego, which he understood in terms of the more dynamic subjectivity, and was influential in using this in relation to sexual difference.

Grosz (1990) has argued that Mitchell's (1974) account of Freudian theory owes an unacknowledged debt to Lacan. Lacan focused upon the relations between women and men, through which he developed a strong theoretical analysis of femininity. His contribution was distinguished by his attention to the importance of *language* as symbolic of structural relations.

Central to his ideas in this context is the notion of the *phallus*. For Lacan, the phallus was distinct from the biological penis, and represented ideas about masculinity in the *symbolic order* under patriarchy. During the post-Oedipus phase, according to Lacan, when the boy identifies with men in general, the penis becomes seen as somehow 'detachable' or a gener alisable phenomenon which represents the masculine. It becomes a 'signifier',[3] not owned by anyone, although available to men rather than women. Girls and women therefore 'identify as the "second sex", as the "other" of men's agency, desire and sexual exchange' (see Sayers, 1986: 86). In Lacan's version of the castration complex, as the child separates from the mother s/he positions her/himself in relation to the mother or father's possession of the imaginary phallus. In other words, the possibility of having a phallus or not (which depends on sex) positions a child in relation to their gender in accord with patriarchal symbolic order.

Through the phallus, each sex is positioned as a speaking being, 'giving reality to the subject'; through the phallus, the *reality* of anatomical sex becomes bound up with the meanings and values that a culture gives to anatomy.

(Grosz, 1990: 131, quoting from Lacan, 1977)

Through possession of the phallus, the subject (male) comes to occupy the position of 'I' in relation to the object 'Other' (female). Masculinity then, is a powerful, active and potent force. The person possessing the phallus is affirmed as the subject who is able to *desire*. Femininity is about acceptance of lack of the phallus and resolution to being the object of that desire. This may only be achieved through the illusion brought about by feminine trappings such as clothing and make-up. These, according to Lacan conceal the 'deficiency' and enable the woman to secure

> access to the phallic. Ironically, in this aim of becoming the object of the other's desire, she becomes the site of a rupture, phallic and castrated, idealised and debased, devoted to the masquerade (an excess) and a deficiency.
>
> (Grosz, 1990: 132)

Thus the woman can be the phallus but only in appearance, because in reality she is not. She can only maintain the masquerade if she is the object of desire.

As Jane Ussher (1995) says:

> This leads to Lacan's apocryphal statement – 'The woman does not exist'. It is a depressing picture – woman is all appearance and sham, or she does not exist at all. Within Lacanian theorising she is all surface and no substance; the misleading object of desire, that promises everything but ultimately offers nothing.
>
> (Ussher, 1995: 2).

However, Ussher goes on to argue that the phallus is also a representation because it is an unattainable phantasy, and although there is little doubt that the symbolic significance of the penis is important, it may be that men fare far worse than women. Having a penis (i.e. being a man) is no indication of warding off the sense of 'lack'. Indeed, lack of the phallus will be felt even more acutely in those who have a penis. Following Frosh (1994), mastery and potency are problematic for men, as individually they have, literally, to measure up to the fantasy of the full phallus (Frosh, 1994: 78, cited in Ussher, 1995).

This is crucial to gender relations in the workplace, particularly in relation to success and failure. Men are socialised into the view that careers have set age-related patterns that progress in a relatively uniform way. They expect to have achieved career success and high status by middle age and for this progression to occur smoothly and 'naturally', and they thus evaluate themselves and others by what they have achieved by the age of 30, 40 and so on. Many women's lives are not like that. They have not been socialised into seeing a career as related to age in this way, and mostly expect their career patterns to be punctuated by periods of part-time work, not working or being home and family oriented. They do not necessarily realise that they may be perceived as having missed the boat and seen as not being a 'high flyer' simply because they have not reached particular career levels at the prescribed age. Men have the potential for power, but more frequently the potential for failure and bitterness. Women have nothing so potent that they need to measure up to, although as the objects, or potential objects, of desire, their energies are exploited and plundered in competing with other women for the right to be the object of a powerful man.

## In summary

The phallus, the symbol of male power, is the inheritance of the male. The phallus enables the man to position himself as the powerful subject, the active, the desirer of the female object. Women may aspire to this by making themselves desirable, but any belief that they possess a phallus is masquerade. Thus there are both male and female ways of looking at the world: one from the position of authority and power, the other from the position of the other, whose only access to power is through being desired, but being desired as a woman with all the implications that femininity brings. Thus in professional life and work organisations, where the climate is competitive, the power resides with possessors of the phallus. However, while all women are excluded, so are some men. It is often the case that these women and men continue to attempt to achieve what they are unaware is the impossible. This results in misuse of energy and finally bitterness. However, as the object of male desire, some women are likely to be perceived as achieving phallic power by unfair means, and the powerless men may turn their bitter energies onto women, which makes the women doubly disadvantaged in terms of their energy expenditure.

The issue of energy and power will be returned to in Parts II and III of the book.

## SEX-TYPED BEHAVIOURS

women have adapted themselves to the wishes of men and felt as if their adaptation were their true nature. That is, they see or saw themselves in the way that their men's wishes demanded of them; unconsciously they yielded to the suggestion of masculine thought.

If we are clear about the extent to which all our being, thinking, and doing conform to these masculine standards, we can see how difficult it is for the individual man and also for the individual woman really to shake off this mode of thought.

(Horney, 1967: 56–57)

Gendered bodies have a meaning and are positioned within the social order. Femininity equates with deficiency and masculinity with power. It is men who set the agenda, they are the 'I', they possess and desire. Women and femininity are defined through this construction of masculinity.

Here I want to reiterate and develop some of the aspects of sex-typed behaviours associated with gender relations in professional life and to place them in the context of biography and the discursive consciousness.

As indicated in the previous chapters, often there is a close link between stereotypical beliefs and what women and men actually do, and believe they should do. As Rhoda Unger suggests (1979), it is likely that 'stereotypes are a component of a larger conceptual process involving how we view the causes of our own and others' behaviour' (Unger, 1979: 51).

Men behave as if they are powerful, or at least heirs to power, almost from the start of life. Women behave as if they are not autonomous and potentially influential beings, but are the objects of the powerful. This is the result of socialisation in the context of patriarchal power relations (Leonard, 1984).

Psychological development, and socialisation into becoming gendered and making sense of gendered behaviour, continue throughout adulthood. Work organisations such as business corporations, town halls, universities, hospitals, legal practices and schools are influential in adult socialisation and provide a powerful context for psychological change.

Women and men entering professions or large companies experience shifts in their subjective experience and their sense of subjectivity/identity through being part of the culture. They see what happens to the people around them – they see who is promoted and who is overlooked. As time passes they evaluate their own progress in relation to others, but also reflexively and discursively monitor their own emotional and behavioural strategies and experience. They cannot, however, do this independent of gender. As Frosh (1992, quoted above), summarised: there are gendered ways of experiencing the world.

What is important, though, is whose view counts, and clearly it is that of *powerful* men. Men are successful if they are able to take the available power. Successful men may be criticised on an interpersonal basis for being selfish, too ambitious, ruthless or underhand. Less successful men also reflect on their experience and some may feel that their masculine status is under threat. However, it is likely that they will have their own means of asserting power, either at home or in their departments over junior staff, nurses, secretaries and female peers. Women are in the paradoxical position of being at risk of losing their femininity if they succeed or are striving to succeed, and also if they fail in their quest for promotion and influence. In both cases they will be seen exhibiting non-feminine behaviour because a successful woman cannot by (patriarchal) definition be nurturant, while someone thwarted in the attempt to achieve success is positioned as bitter, competitive and envious because they do not have essential ingredients to fulfil themselves. This is not feminine because 'little girls are not like that'. Femininity is about *accepting the lack*. Anything short of that is perversion and neurosis.

However, it is not only psychoanalytic theorists who have addressed the issues surrounding the beliefs and behaviours surrounding masculinity and femininity. As Bem (1974) began to suggest in the mid-1970s, the notion that femininity and masculinity are static qualities that only apply to attributes demonstrated by biological females or males, is absurd. Her concern with research on stereotypical gendered behaviours focused on women's and men's abilities to employ different characteristics according to circumstances. This meant that men could play the active, masculine, aggressive role on the rugby field, but exhibit tenderness and gentle behaviour towards, for example, babies and kittens. Women were able to be assertive or nurturant when the situation demanded. Sandra Bem further stressed the centrality of androgynous qualities such as intellect, honesty and interpersonal competence qualities in all people. She made the assumption that it was possible for men and women to operate primarily in an androgynous way.

However, separating femininity and masculinity from biology, and using them, along with androgyny, as concepts which relate to personality and behaviour, meant that she side-stepped the problems of gendered power and inequality and thus the meaning of femininity and masculinity. Alison Thomas, (1985, 1986) argues that Bem's contribution is limited.

> Bem offers no satisfactory way of independently ascertaining the meaning of the person's gender-schema . . . Bem has in fact overlooked an important cognitive issue – namely, whether or not her subjects actually share her own definitions of femininity and masculinity as represented in the Bem Sex Role Inventory.
>
> (Thomas, 1985: 2)

Thomas herself suggests that gender has a meaning for each of us, individually and collectively. She extends the notion of gender character-istics by raising questions about the interpretation of traditional feminine qualities. Thus, in a critique of Bem, she states:

> What, critically, is not taken into account is whether or not the person concerned, describing herself, perhaps as 'nurturant', actually shares

Bem's view that this is a feminine trait and sees it as relevant to herself. If she does not...then any inference about her self-perceived femininity is rendered invalid. She may indeed appear feminine, as judged by normative standards, but whether she construes herself as feminine or not cannot be established without first finding out her own constructions of what is or is not 'feminine'. This is where it becomes necessary to acknowledge the importance of personal representations of gender, and specifically, ideologies of gender, in any serious attempt to understand what gender means in self-perception. In other words, to consider the political along with the personal.

(Thomas, 1986: 4)

Thomas' own work demonstrates that beliefs about gender and self-concept are complex. Individual women and men *do* operate reflexively and gender is a crucial aspect of their personal biographies. However, she has arguably focused too heavily on the cognitive aspects of gender schemas and masculinity and femininity, at the expense of social experience and intersubjectivity.

As Mead (1934), social constructionists (from phenomenological sociologists such as Berger and Kellner (1964), through Harré (1993) and Shotter (1995), to psychological discourse analysts such as Potter and Wetherell (1987)) and psychoanalytic theorists (Freud, 1973; Lacan, 1977) have all stressed, society/social discourses 'pre-exist' the individual in some way, and the process of living as a gendered person is not one of choice. The body, language and power relationships all conspire against volition.

## GENDER–POWER RELATIONSHIPS

In a game where you cannot win, the sensible thing to do is to refuse to play.
(Breakwell, 1985: 118)

Power relations are both intentional and nonsubjective. If in fact they are intelligible, this is not because they are the effect of another instance that 'explains' them, but rather because they are imbued, through and through, with calculation: there is no power that is exercised without a series of aims and objectives. But this does not mean it results from the choice of an individual subject.

(Foucault, 1978: 94–95)

Participants in social interactions are aware of the fact that power is a crucial part of the dynamic, that it resides with individuals within the social organisation, and that those with the power will maintain their influence (Bell and Newby, 1976). Most formal and informal meetings – at home, socially and in work organisations involve some degree of power acknowledgement and response. Some individuals walk away from struggles for power, particularly if they know they will not win. Others feel the obligation to dent the power of others in some small way.

Women and men at work know that they have to respond or negotiate around the rules set by the senior members of the company. Some individuals, however, are more personally powerful than others, a fact noted several years ago by social psychologists (French and Raven, 1959). They identified different forms of power: power that comes with the job (i.e. being the senior manager), power which comes with individual charisma, power connected with specific forms of knowledge, and power associated with experience of particular situations.

There is a tension between social science perspectives on gender–power relations and the 'objective' notion of power, where the focus is upon the fact that certain attributes are valued more highly than others. From this perspective, gender inequality is simply the result of social norms, which are potentially changeable (for example in the work of sex-role theorists such as Sandra Bem).

The 'subjective/interactive' perspective on the other hand, involves unravelling the meaning of gendered interactions. It involves taking account of the *relationship* between men and women as well as their characteristics and their roles in society (as in the work of Peter Leonard or Wendy Hollway).

Gender relations are the site for power struggles and power-based conflicts in work organisations as well as in the domestic sphere. Power remains firmly in the hands of (some) men, although not without resistance from other men and women.

Foucault has argued that power and knowledge are equivalent, and the fact that men have traditionally been the ones to define what is and is not knowledge has ensured power stability. Patriarchal knowledge has defined women and men, femininity and masculinity, and as such has limited the discourses available through which to understand gender–power relations as distinct from the model in which women are subordinate and men are superordinate (Leonard, 1984).

## CONCLUSIONS

Although things may be changing for women under patriarchy, the price for attainment of professional success is high. Women in their pursuit and achievement of power stand to lose their subjective sense of femininity, the sense of being a woman, their creative energy and peace of mind. Men continue to retain their advantages, and although many do mentor women and openly support equal opportunities in a variety of ways, this has not led to a real shift in the gender–power balance, but only to some women gaining success.

Why do men appear to take up women's causes at work if in the end it might shift the power balance? Why do women persist in their attempts to enter the male bastions of power in the workplace when the cost is so great?

The answer lies in the relationship between women and men and the way in which power evolves and is managed. The decision for a woman to enter a profession, and to distinguish herself in some way from other women, has ensured either a 'fight to the death' or an opting out (which may in fact be the same thing). Although power is constant, in that relationships are always between superordinate and subordinate individuals and groups, the form is fluid. Power relations are not inevitable, unchanging or unalterable (Faith, 1994).

## NOTES

1   Horney believed that infants are aware of sex differences from the very start of life (see Sayers, 1986: 37).
2   This is a crude and far from complete account of the Oedipal crisis and the development of the superego. For details of this, see Freud (1925).
3   Lacan (1977) argued that the 'sign' (the smallest unit of analysis in semiotics) is situated internally to the subject within the realm of thought. This means that the 'signifier' (material, phonic component) refers to any given 'signified' (conceptual component) through the mediation of a language with no fixed anchor point (cf. Saussure, 1974, who considered that there was a fixed core of language).

# Professional socialisation and patriarchal culture

Put into historical
context.
generation to generation;
an ongoing brawl

331.4/HAC
331.42/MAC
331.4/GEN
301.4/GEN
331.4094/DAU
331.4133094/WOM
331.4/WOM

# Introduction to Part II

[Organisational cultures are generally created by men and therefore have male interests at heart. To this extent cultural processes actually work against women and serve to re-inforce their organisational powerlessness. This powerlessness reflects the distribution of power in society at large. In this sense culture mirrors social reality. Therefore through the process of the production of organisational culture, gender differences in organisations are reproduced.

(Cassell and Walsh, 1991: 4)]

Even though interaction between society and self occurs from the earliest time in a person's life (Mead, 1934; Leonard, 1984; and see Chapter 2), socialisation (the transmission of cultural values from one generation to the next) is a continuing process throughout the life cycle. Society and its social institutions are microcosmic representations of wider cultural contexts which are hierarchical and patriarchal, and entering professional life is akin to the more general socialisation process.

Entry into an organisation or a profession is the beginning of a specific socialisation, and professional organisations operate to ensure that new members are aware of the rules and values that ensure the perpetuation of the dominant culture of that organisation and group. That is not to say that cultures are intractable or inescapable, nor that individuals and groups never resist socialisation. However, the cultural mores of the organisation pre-exist the individual employee and operate to restrict entry, career progress and to influence behaviour in all spheres of the operation of the organisational culture.

In Part I I examined the complex interaction between human knowledge, reflexivity and the unconscious in the social construction of femininity and masculinity. I argued that all these features of human experience serve towards an individual sense of gendered biography.

In Part II the focus is upon how our gendered biographies enable us to relate to and resist professional socialisation in patriarchal organisations.

It raises questions about how women and men interact with each other in an organisational context, and what characteristics of that organisational context and the biographical profiles of its gendered constituents aid the gender–power imbalance in favour of men.

[Entry into a male-dominated organisation is likely to be a severe culture shock for women at the start of their careers, so much so that sometimes they may fail to perceive the extent of male domination, which occurs at different levels of visibility and strengths of voracity.]

The psychological consequences of patriarchy for professional women are potentially pathological and possibly detrimental to health. This is both for indirect reasons such as ignoring women's special needs in relation to domestic commitments and traditional styles of social interaction, and direct reasons such as overt sexism and sexual harassment. This 'toxic context' constrains women's experience, and although some women achieve success, they pay a dearer price for this than their male equivalents.

For women there are three main stages of socialisation into patriarchal organisational culture:

1   *Shock* on entry into the system, which frequently occurs in delayed stages, because of a previous lack of awareness of sexism resulting from school success, high motivation and an idealised view of their potential (as with the medical students discussed in Chapter 2). This shock frequently leads to:

2   *Anger* and/or *protest* and a decision to leave, or the development of a coping strategy or a compromise, which is referred to as gender management strategies (Cassell and Walsh, 1991; Marshall, 1984, 1994). The decision to leave might be masked (consciously or unconsciously) by a decision to have children or focus on the family, or to work part time, thereby 'dropping out' of the fast-track rat race.

3   *Internalisation of values.* This process – the ultimate acceptance of the patriarchal culture – operates differently for the women who opt out than for those who opt in. The former group re-evaluate themselves negatively against the criteria. Thus they might say that 'family comes first', or 'women aren't made for the pressures of senior management', or 'I have failed', or even 'who wants to work with such people in that way?'. The second group, who choose to take up the challenge of patriarchy, are the future Queen Bees who see themselves as the exceptions to the rules that subordinate and disparage women (see Marshall, 1984; White et al., 1992; McKenzie Davey, 1993).]

However, all women, however successful, operate within the toxic context, and in the three chapters that follow I provide evidence of the dangers of patriarchal organisations in more detail.

Chapter 4, 'Gender at work', begins by exploring the differences between socialisation into masculinity and femininity and how these patterns are maintained in the course of professional socialisation. It will provide specific case examples of gendered behaviour among professional groups, focusing upon the way that emotional, interpersonal and organisational forces at all levels of consciousness conspire to reinforce these patterns.

Chapter 5, 'In the shadow of the glass ceiling', begins from the perspective of the patriarchal culture and suggests the ways in which men potentially thrive in this climate to the detriment of their female colleagues. It again examines the different levels of consciousness at which patriarchy and individuals and groups interact, and case examples will be provided as illustration.

Chapter 6, 'Sexuality, power and organisation', identifies the way that male sexuality underlies the patriarchal culture of professional life. This occurs in both overt and covert ways, but, more importantly, it is taken for granted as a normal and healthy way of life. Women's sexuality and women's bodies are the objects of masculine attention and derision, and these processes reinforce the objectification of women, serving to hinder their progress as a professional.

Thus Part II of this book provides a conceptual bridge between the continuing fact of discrimination by men and patriarchal organisations against women's success, and the changing context in which these changes and the ensuing backlash interplay.

While women are increasingly gaining a profile as high-flying managers, businesswomen and professionals, organisational cultures remain largely hostile to women's advancement and control. A 'good' organisation is seen to be one in which concessions are made through equal opportunities and other policies. However, none of these reparations take effect without resistance and derision from many men and some women.

The 'toxic context' of the patriarchal organisation permits equal opportunities policies but resists changes that enable women and other minority groups to have the same opportunities as those available to men. Professional organisations, top-heavy with men, frequently pay lip service to increasing the recruitment and promotion opportunities for women. However, the existence of such 'policies' makes it more difficult for women either to negotiate their careers or to challenge the 'system'. It is currently fashionable to deride feminism and what may be referred to as humourless 'political correctness'. Young women with good qualifications and expectations of career success firmly believe they have reached the 'post-feminist' utopia which will enable their efforts to be judged on merit rather than on gender, and feminist critiques or actions are seen as lacking in 'style' and relevance (see Faludi, 1992).

The focus in Part II will be on how successful professional women negotiate their careers, and will draw on their experiences of 'being a woman, not a man'.

# Chapter 4

# Gender at work

## INTRODUCTION

As argued in Chapter 3, the inner psyche and the social world are structured on clear gendered lines, and there is an intrinsic link between gender and experience. Women and men, boys and girls, have implicit knowledge of how this works. This rule applies regardless of whether one takes a behaviourist, cognitive developmental, social constructionist or psychoanalytic perspective.

Here, I examine gender socialisation and assess the way gendered behaviours and experiences are 'transferred' from the family to the workplace, with this 'spillover' held together through biography, reflexivity and unconscious processes.

## GENDER ROLE DEVELOPMENT

In Part I it became clear that despite the best efforts of liberal feminists, gender role socialisation and stereotypical role expectations remain an integral part of human experience (Bleier, 1984). In observing studies of gender role socialisation for girls and boys, John Archer (1989) has argued that 'The most striking feature is the separation of their social worlds, entailing two different cultures' (1989: 367). If this is the case, and there is increasing evidence that this is so, it is not surprising that women and men adopt different patterns of behaviours and enjoy differential sets of expertise. However, difference – even when this signifies underlying resonance with the subordination of women, as argued in Chapter 3 – may be subject to resistance, which has implications for effectiveness and achievement in work organisations.

To understand the ways in which women and men operate at the organisational level, however, it is useful to examine gender socialisation and the differences between the experiences and expectations of girls and boys.

Archer (1986, 1989) has made the case that gender role development is not simply the result of differential socialisation. The basis of femininity and masculinity underlying the socialisation process is qualitatively different. Boys, from an early age, are under pressure to conform to their gender roles; which contrasts markedly with the experience of girls. Boys are also pressured to maintain a sharp distinction between their interaction with other boys and with girls, limiting their relationships with the latter.

How does this work? There appear to be two main sources of pressure: the punishment of femininity in boys and the elevation of masculinity, and thus other boys, as manifesting a superior form of development.

## Different pathways

> Masculinity is like a club, entry to which boys can gain in different degrees. The general requirements for entry centre on not being a sissy and on being tough.
> (Archer, 1989: 368)

There is abundant evidence from studies of developmental psychology that boys are more likely to be punished if they exhibit 'feminine' behaviour, while little attention is given to girls' transgressions of this type. Girls are indulged or ignored if they wear cowboy or spacemen suits but boys are not equally treated if they wear make-up or high heeled shoes (Bee, 1981). There appears to be more anxiety about the possibility of a boy being a 'sissy' than of girls behaving like 'tomboys'. The former is seen as so problematic that it has been identified in the United States as a 'childhood gender disturbance' (Archer, 1986, 1989). Masculinity, which Archer argues is both more complex and contradictory than femininity, is characterised by rigid role requirements in childhood. By this he meant that more is expected of boys during childhood, but in particular they learn to avoid the feminine. During this time, girls are relatively free. The female role however, becomes less flexible in adolescence, which 'can be viewed as a way of marking out both the subordination of women and their value as a sexual and reproductive commodity for men' (Archer, 1989: 369).

Across the life span, however, particularly because of childbirth and motherhood, females have a far greater degree of change than do males (Archer, 1986).

Archer illustrates this through popular culture, citing, for instance, *The Beano* (a UK children's comic), which depicts the different range of expectations permissible for girls and the limits to those for boys. 'Minnie the Minx' 'is a positive character who climbs trees and plays masculine sports, "Softy Walter" (in the "Dennis the Menace" comic strip) is an object of ridicule who associates with girls, has feminine interests such as dolls and musical boxes, lacks toughness, and cries' (Archer, 1989: 368). In Enid Blyton's *Famous Five*, 'George' (really Georgina) claims she can do anything that Dick and Julian can do, and her behaviour is contrasted with the more traditionally feminine Anne. As Archer points out, being a tomboy may give a girl enhanced status. This situation for girls is not as clear-cut as Archer maintains though, and although there is a limited status for the tomboy, there are increasing sanctions as the girl reaches puberty. Even for young girls, the role models of George and Minnie as tomboys do not have the autonomy and power of real boys. The 'problems' of femininity become apparent well before adolescence (see Nicolson, 1991a).

## Gender boundaries

As boys become socialised into masculinity, they gradually become segregated from their female peers. 'Boys' games' emerge, which exclude sisters and former friends, and these games coincide with the distinction of masculinity from 'other' behaviours. Richmal Crompton's *Just William* books again provide good illustrations of this. William and his friends, 'The Outlaws', have sisters and know girls from school, but a constant theme is the fear of being made to play with girls. At certain times one member of The Outlaws may have a secretly good experience or feeling about being with a particular girl, but they always find a way to overcome this and return to the 'real' world of boys. One of their worst fears is spending time with Violet Elizabeth Bott, the ultra-feminine child who uses her femininity ('I'll scream and I'll scream until I'm sick' – said with a lisp!) to persuade them to allow her to join them. While she wants to play with them, their project is to avoid her – they would never want to manipulate their way into joining girls.

However, this does not coincide fully with the empirical work which suggests that boys 'spoil' girls' games. Thorne (1986), cited by Archer, has suggested that gendered play is like a contest and includes 'pollution rituals' where one side or the other is able to contaminate the rivals. Thorne observed that girls tend to be more likely to be invaded/polluted by boys, which leads to girls having defensive tactics such as chasing boys away or telling adults (or screaming till they are sick).

There is, if nothing else, an ambivalence on the part of pre-adolescent

boys towards their female peers. Archer concludes that this is because of
the social importance placed on the masculine role, and although the
emphasis varies during the course of childhood and adolescent development, flexibility for boys is only permissible once the masculine role has
been clearly transmitted.

## Reproduction of mothering

Masculinity is about independence and autonomy; femininity is about co-
operative behaviours, nurturance and dependence (Broverman et al.,
1970; see also Chapter 3). Archer's analysis of the development of gender
roles assumes the imperative towards cultural transmission through a
system of direct reward – and punishment for violation – at various stages
of development. This occurs through the traditional channels of socialisation: the family, peer group, school (Weitzman, 1979), and as Archer
points out, upholds the privileging of masculinity and boys and men. .

It is the mother who is the primary agent of childhood development
and socialisation within the family. This fact reiterates complex questions
about how the subordination of women and the supremacy of masculinity
and the male role are reproduced in the family, and consequently in the
workplace, which is reminiscent of Freud's view (see Chapter 3).

Chodorow (1978), the American sociologist and psychoanalyst, has
been influential in explaining this apparent paradox, although not
without challenge. As she asserts it is *women* who *mother*, a responsibility
with which they are charged based on their abilities to give birth, lactate
and thus feed infants. Many feminists would argue that this is where the
biological imperative should end, although it clearly does not (Bleier,
1984).

As a sociologist, Chodorow argues that a woman's role as a mother
enjoys a high profile now because, through economic development and
the consequent division of labour in western capitalist societies, mothering has 'ceased to be embedded in a range of other activities and human
relations. It stands out in its emotional intensity and meaning, and its
centrality for women's lives and social definition' (Chodorow, 1978: 6).
Even prior to industrialisation and the genesis of the bourgeois family
though, there is little to persuade the observer that child care was the
province of men, or even a shared role. So why do women continue to
take the primary child-care responsibility, and in so doing do they
continue to reproduce the traditional mothering role in the next
generation?

It is as a psychoanalyst rather than sociologist that Chodorow makes her theoretical contribution to the debate on the reproduction of mothering. According to Chodorow, within the context of patriarchy, women's mothering is causally related to the way child care and the division of labour have evolved. Contemporary mothering is about concern for others, nurturance, vigilance and dependence on a bread-winner. It is, however, *not* about ambition, intellect and competitiveness. The psychological capacities which underlie gendered child-rearing tasks are thus reproduced both consciously and unconsciously from generation to generation.

> Women as mothers, produce daughters with mothering capacities and the desire to mother. These capacities and needs are built into and grow out of the mother–daughter relationship itself. By contrast, women as mothers (and men as not-mothers) produce sons whose nurturant capacities and needs have been systematically curtailed and suppressed.
>
> (Chodorow, 1978: 7)

But how does this happen? By definition, patriarchal culture oppresses women, particularly through the motherhood role, when women experience loss of self and autonomy to an extreme extent. Chodorow, aware of the contradictions inherent in the practice of selfless mothering, suggests that part of women's/mothers' behaviour is to try to meet needs that cannot be met through relationships with adult men and women, through their relationship with the infant/child. This is different in relation to sons than it is for daughters. Mothers demand different things from children depending on their sex – sons are expected to be substitute husbands, while daughters are treated as substitute mothers. Masculinity and independence are fostered in sons, who feel pressure to separate psychologically from their mothers, and who thus emerge from their pre-Oedipal attachment with the desire to assert their masculinity through the domination of women. There is less conflict for girls, and femininity and nurturance are encouraged and sustained in daughters (Chodorow, 1978: 212).

Sayers (1982) suggests that in effect Chodorow is saying that gender identity equates with personality 'style'. Sayers also shows that Chodorow's work has been used politically to reinforce the centrality of mothering to child care.

Crucial to this discussion of the emergence of gendered behaviours and emotions is the strength of *emotional segregation* between women and men, which is encapsulated in the work of both Archer and Chodorow, despite their very different perspectives.

## FEMININITY AT WORK

How then may we understand gendered behaviour at work? Debates about biological essentialism vs. socialisation and behavioural learning, and psychoanalysis and the meaning of the gendered body vs. liberal feminism, have neither been resolved nor have they evaporated. What is clear from consideration of the literature on femininity, masculinity and gender roles is that biology, social context, ideology and the experience of being a gendered person all contribute towards understanding professional socialisation and the culture of organisations.

### Sex-role spillover

Sex-role spillover seems inescapable for many women regardless of their seniority. This process occurs in two ways. First, where the skills, expectations and behaviours which women employ in managing their domestic and family lives are also used at work; and second, when professional women have to deal with the strains of managing their dual roles.

As Davidson and Cooper (1992) outline, all managers have home and work roles and responsibilities but women report more stress than do men. This is true at all stages of the life cycle, regardless of marriage and parenthood, as in fact female managers are less likely to have children than male managers. Whereas for a man marriage and a family are experienced as an asset ensuring stability, for a woman it is a potential burden (see Davidson and Cooper, 1992).

Underlying these gender differences in experience are the assumptions about the roles of 'wife' and 'mother'. For men they indicate the provision of comfort and support, but for women they mean two sets of overlapping responsibilities. As the domestic roles of women often circumscribe their characteristic repertoires, this role overlap has major implications for the way they manage the competing aspects of their lives. Illustration of how this may operate on a fundamental level can be seen through looking at the motherhood role.

Women are socialised into motherhood within the traditional feminine role, which does not simply mean that they desire to be mothers. It means that they desire to become mothers *in a particular way*: they want to become 'perfect' mothers.

A prevalent and popular theme in psychology and psychoanalysis over the last twenty years has reinforced the view that mothers, through their inability to fulfil the total needs of the infant and family, are to blame for psychological problems in the next generation (see Sayers, 1992). This view is both potentially misogynistic and also indicative of a sense of omnipotence on the part of the mothers who accept this charge and feel so responsible. Thus:

> mothers are totally responsible for the outcomes of their mothering, even if their behaviour in turn is shaped by male-dominant society. Belief in the all-powerful mother spawns a recurrent tendency to blame the mother on the one hand, and a fantasy of maternal perfectibility on the other.
>
> (Chodorow and Contratto, 1982: 55)

From this, Chodorow and Contratto extrapolate that women come to see themselves as responsible for everything from men's bad behaviour to the unmet needs of all children. This theme of the perfect mother comes to provide a template for women's behaviour, emotionality and for the standards they set themselves in the public sphere. If we take from both the sex-role learning perspective of John Archer and the psychoanalytic framework employed by Nancy Chodorow, it is clear that while femininity has potentially fluid boundaries at early stages of girls' development, it is soon constrained by motherhood practices, both in that women who work are or are likely to become mothers and that women are not expected to engage in the kinds of behaviour that would in any way be deemed 'unmotherly'.

As girls are socialised into expecting to be mothers on the conscious level, they anticipate their role so that it is assured of becoming integral to their repertoire. On the unconscious level, girls identify with their own mothers and women in general, and thus mothering has become incorporated into expectations and beliefs about women's 'styles' and work-related roles.

## The role of academic women: a case study

At a recent workshop run by feminist psychologists (Woollett et al., 1995), attended (incidentally) exclusively by women and set up to explore women's experiences in academic psychology, the following issues, supporting the view that women engage in sex-role spillover, became clear .

First, women have *expectations of themselves* which correspond to some extent with the traditional roles of females and mothers but that are inappropriate in patriarchal settings. Interactions with students made this clear. Women academics have to *teach themselves* not to be responsible for their students' potential misery or failures, which is not the same as the negligence of student needs operationalised by some colleagues.

I recalled a recent example of my relationship with a female postgraduate who was completing her PhD – a typically stressful experience for both parties! She had requested to see me to discuss an aspect of the final draft that was worrying her, and we met to discuss it for around one and a half hours. The following week the same student phoned to say that although she had appreciated my willingness to discuss her work, she had been too anxious to concentrate fully and so asked whether we could meet again. I agreed, as I liked her and was keen that she should finish her thesis, which had great promise. However, I felt extremely resentful as soon as I had done so. The second meeting we had, as with the previous one, seemed to me to be effective but did not diffuse her worries. This left me feeling that my skills as a supervisor were somehow inadequate, but I was angry with myself for feeling that way as I knew it was untrue. I was also angry with her for not valuing my time on either occasion, and also appearing to devalue the high quality of attention she had had from me over the preceding years.

The problem here lies with the interaction and expectations which both took for granted, which need now to be problematised. I choose my graduate students on the basis that I like them and am interested in their work, and reserve the option to turn down those applicants who do not match these criteria. This corresponds with female academic behaviours observed by Maaret Wager (1995), in which women academics describe their work almost as a hobby. It also corresponds with the behaviour of mothers who freely give time and attention to their children, which is fine when the mother is feeling strong, able and willing to give – which may be much of the time. However, it is impossible for the child or student to recognise times when these conditions do not apply, which brings about a serious mismatch. What has happened is a failure – in this case on my part (as mother/teacher/supervisor) to set adequate boundaries in advance.

The second issue that arose from this workshop was that these expectations of 'woman as mother' are *reciprocated* by colleagues and students, who expect female academics to be 'motherly'. This is true in the example I have just given, but arose in the workshop in relation to teaching undergraduates. Students appear to find it easier to knock on the door of the female academic for advice or material, rather than approach a male staff member. Several colleagues report, for instance, that a common excuse students give for disturbing them was 'I need to get in touch with Dr X (male colleague) but as he is so busy, perhaps I could ask you ... '.

Third, ambitious behaviour in relation to academic careers is seen as problematic. This is characteristic of the experience of all female professionals and an important issue in the management and negotiation of the professional role. An assertive, forthright woman is seen as aggressive or 'over the top', which is not true for men exhibiting the same behaviour and is not acceptable in 'mothering'. Typical of women in many academic departments is that they either become positioned as the aggressive harridans or they keep their heads down and get on with their work. If they are invisible, they are acceptable in the academy. If they do achieve, then jokes may be made about their use of sexuality to gain favours from senior men (see Chapter 6), but rarely is a woman academic seen to have achieved on the basis of her work.

Fourth, women academics seem to have an overdeveloped *sense of responsibility* in relation to their work, which resonates with the fantasy of the perfect mother described above – they set out to achieve the impossible in relation to the quality and quantity of their research and their teaching.

Despite the student–lecturer power relationship having potential child–mother parallels, women in the academic context are not 'typically' feminine in any sense. Scholarship and research is not seen as typical of female behaviour, so it is no surprise that only 3 per cent of professors in UK universities are women (Aziz, 1990). European countries, Canada and the USA have similar proportions in the senior echelons of academia (Wager, 1995).

### The culture trap

It is obvious that a great deal of sex role learning takes place among women during the early phases of their lives, and that this can translate itself into an attitude of mind that creates difficulties later in worklife generally. This we have called 'the culture trap'.

(Davidson and Cooper, 1992: 56)

What is 'normal' feminine behaviour? For women in the professions and management there are few same-sex role models for them to learn from, and there are clear problems in trying to emulate men. An enduring debate among feminists as suggested in the previous chapters has centred around the idea of *essential* femininity, and Carol Gilligan's (1982) work on female morality has been correctly criticised for failing to problematise the distinction she found between female and male 'styles' (Faludi, 1992). Similarly much has been said in favour of women managers and female management style, relying on the assumption that it is fairer and more democratic than male style. However, while gender differences must not be ignored, they have to be understood in context if inequality is to be recognised and changes made. It needs to be admitted that in the world of business and the professions, typical female behaviour is not valued by those with power. Nor is it seen as effective in terms of organisational and professional goals.

Flanders (1994) argues that 'Whereas male managers tend to have one role – that of the traditional stereotyped manager, there are many different roles that women can adopt' (p. 68). This echoes John Archer's thesis about gender role development, in which as shown above in this chapter, there is a lack of clarity about femininity. This makes it more difficult for a woman to enter a man's world because not only has she not had socialisation into 'masculinity', which arguably corresponds with what is expected of managers and senior professionals, but she may be unclear about her own sense of 'femininity' as she is not primarily a mother.

Flanders indicates that many women thus adopt inappropriate roles which resemble stereotypical female ones, which in themselves may be problematic in other contexts.

These include 'the mother confessor'. In such a role the senior woman offers a shoulder to cry on. This is time-consuming and emotionally tiring and may lead to conflict in carrying out the executive role (Cassell and Walsh, 1991).

Another possibility is the 'departmental mascot', a fate which often also befalls a token woman (see Davidson and Cooper, 1992): the 'departmental tea lady', who is asked to take minutes at meetings in the secretary's absence, or literally make tea; the 'bridesmaid' who acts in relation to her senior manager as if she were a personal assistant and thus indispensable; the 'seductress', who engages in a mild flirtation in order to get noticed or because this is the major pattern she has developed to relate to men; and finally 'the feminist' who is seen as strident, aggressive and anti-male.

However, most professional women have been made, or made themselves, aware of these obvious pitfalls. Many of the women doctors I interviewed commented how they were initially expected to do the equivalent of make tea on the wards, but that they soon made it clear that they were not prepared to do this. Many senior women managers never reveal their ability to type, despite its obvious use in a variety of contexts.

The message that might be construed from such a list of potential pitfalls – namely, to avoid making these mistakes – is not an easy one to respond to. Women who are ambitious wish to be both visible and indistinguishable from male colleagues with whom they want to compete on the basis of professional merit alone.

## Women at the top

Kate McKenzie Davey (1993) carried out an interview study with women graduates early in their management career to examine how they coped with issues of femininity. She found ambivalence and conflict in the interview material, although the overt message was positive. Much of her data revealed the differences between women's and men's perceptions of good practice in management. Women see men's styles as different from and less acceptable than their own.

> They, men, seem to be terrific backbiters . . . back-stabbers is perhaps a better word and I come across it where a man has tried to stab me in the back and I think, but why?
>
> (McKenzie Davey, 1993: 9)

Another of her respondents reinforced this point. 'I don't want to be like them, I don't want to play the game like they do' (McKenzie Davey, 1993: 9).

Women do expect something different of themselves. Many find that although they might reject traditional female roles, they are able to save something of their femininity by adapting it to the management context.

Geraldine McCool, the solicitor mentioned in Chapter 2, said she ran her department in a way that differed from male management style.

> In her current appointment she continues to draw upon the lessons she learned in those early years. As a young woman in charge of a department she had the sense to combine instinct with wide consultation 'Although I often responded to my gut reactions I never took irrevocable action until I had spoken to everyone whose opinion was relevant. This gave me the confidence of knowing that my decisions were well informed'. She believes that management is about ensuring commitment from others. 'This can only be achieved if there is emphasis on teamwork and the people doing the work are involved in decisions'. She thinks that, as a rule, managers should not keep information from staff. 'Even if you come to a decision they do not agree with, at least they will know why something has occurred.'
>
> (Nicolson, 1995 c: 30)

On the other side of the coin are senior women who try to be like men or at least avoid taking a woman-oriented position. My own research with female academics and clinical consultants (Nicolson and Welsh, 1994) revealed little empathy for the day-to-day discrimination that juniors had to face. One female consultant, talking of sexual harassment, said:

> Men are in the main responsible for sexual harassment. There are large numbers of women working in less powerful positions in the health service. They need to be encouraged to object to such behaviour.
>
> (Female, 41, paediatrics)

This comment showed little awareness of her own position of authority and potential influence, ignoring the cost to a junior woman of complaining about a senior colleague in a hierarchical profession when personal recommendation in appointments and promotion counts for a great deal. Another, again talking of sexual harassment, confirmed her own capabilities and inferred the inadequacies of those who could not handle this kind of male behaviour.

> A professor of a surgical department made a stupid (but nasty) remark in an otherwise serious meeting, designed to put me down and prevent me arguing for a particular option. Pointless, silly, off-putting, no sexual approach intended, but simply to put me off my stride. It didn't.
>
> (Female clinical academic in her forties)

Senior women in the sample overall tended to demonstrate similar attitudes when they claimed an awareness of harassment and discrimination. The junior women and men looked to support from those in authority to stop discrimination. The senior women considered it had to be handled on one's own and was not serious.

However, McKenzie Davey's sample of younger women graduates in management suggested more reflexivity about the dominance of men and how to cope with it. One engineer said that she had

> become one of the lads and that can be quite easy because again you ... drink a pint or two, you talk laddish things and ... that's the only way that some men can relate to women.
>
> (McKenzie Davey, 1993: 10)

Two other women actively acknowledged the need to play by men's rules in order to survive but, unlike the older medical women, neither was happy with this. One said 'I'm not saying it's the best way, but I've got to look at it that way' (McKenzie Davey, 1993: 11), and the other 'Perhaps I'm learning these men's rules ... I don't know ... but I haven't got confidence in them'(ibid., p. 11).

Jane McLoughlin's businesswomen, discussed in Chapter 2, were also aware of the tension between men's and women's rules. Some demonstrated this by competing with men and not women.

At the start of my career, I felt very competitive with men. I felt I did the work as well as they did. I still feel more competitive with men than with women. I felt proud at beating men, and that was an incentive to keep pushing forward.

(McLoughlin, 1992: 112)

This was also true for women bosses:

I've always got along well with the women who work for me, but I handle them by saying, 'Watch me and do as I do'. I've never thrown my weight around except with men, because men challenged me much more. I've never felt competition with people below me, but I've had desperately hard times competing with men above me.

(McLoughlin, 1992: 112)

This is reminiscent of the work of Thorne (1986), discussed earlier in this chapter, in relation to girls' defensive behaviour towards boys who try to disrupt their play. As the traditional adversary, boys (and men) are fair game, and the habits of early development die hard.

Women know how to be women and how to work with women like themselves. But being a woman at present remains marginal to the commercial and professional world – a successful woman has to be more than herself. Women's lives, circumscribed by gender roles and power relations, mean that women bring different sets of experiences to their work. Patriarchal cultures tend to overlook the strengths women's life experiences potentially bring to business and professional life (Smith, 1978). The culture trap is not only about the 'limitations' of women's attitudes and behaviour, but is about the way these are positioned as marginal to a patriarchal context.

## Women in pursuit of success: organisational roles

What is typical of the successful woman? Is it someone who pretends to be a man or at least attempts to behave as if she were gender-free like the senior doctors? That there are few role models or precedents is generally seen to disadvantage women climbing the career ladder. How does a feminine but ambitious woman behave? Can a woman work happily with men and avoid the pitfalls mentioned by Flanders above?

Not all successful women see the absence of predecessors as a problem.

Janet Finch, interviewed prior to taking over as Vice-chancellor at the University of Keele in the autumn of 1995, argues:

> 'Because there isn't a role model of a woman manager in universities, in many ways you can define the role yourself. That creates opportunities. . . . I am clear about what I want to do, I am straightforward, so it is easy for people to disagree with me. It has brought me into conflict with people, most of whom are men'. Her advice to women contemplating a management career is 'not to be put off by the lack of other women', but try to find mentors, and make contact with women in similar positions of seniority.
>
> (*Times Higher Education Supplement* (*THES*), 28 July 1995: 19)

Elizabeth Esteve-Coll, who at the same time succeeded as Vice-chancellor of the University of East Anglia, challenges the view that women operate along gendered lines:

> It is a generally held view that women rule by emotion, which is pejorative, or that they rule by intuition which is intended as praise, but nobody can manage a large complex organisation, the size of a small town in some cases, with responsibility for many millions of pounds on the basis of intuition.
>
> (*THES*, 28 July 1995: 19)

The third new vice-chancellor to take up a post (making five the total number of women vice-chancellors in UK universities), Christine King, had been the first Chair of the Glass Ceiling network for university managers. She believes that women do things differently:

> There is an excitement and an expectation of a change of culture at the university with my vice-chancellorship. I would like to think we can do things in a different way. A woman is an outsider in the world of university hierarchies and in a sense that legitimates differences and opens up other possibilities and approaches.
>
> I am very committed to team work as I think many women are. Building effective teams means allowing people to claim success in their areas of strength. I would favour training schemes giving opportunities to women and a woman-only staff monitoring scheme, but I am not in favour of quotas. There is nothing worse than the wrong woman in the wrong job, everybody suffers when that happens.
>
> (*THES*, 28 July 1995: 19)

Each of these women takes a slightly different position on the issue of gender, but each of them clearly believes that women who achieve senior status deserve to do so. None appears to feel that power and influence are detrimental to their femininity, but all feel they are being assessed as senior *women* rather than as other vice-chancellors.

## MASCULINITY AT WORK

A critical analysis of men and masculinities is particularly important in the study of work, organisations and management. Yet an examination of the available literature reveals a recurring paradox. The categories of men and masculinity are frequently central to the analyses, yet they remain taken for granted, hidden and unexamined.

(Collinson and Hearn, 1994: 3)

Since the executive role is usually perceived by both men and women as fundamentally a male role, any individual woman manager is unlikely to be seen as adequately fitting or meeting the role requirements.

(Davidson and Cooper, 1992: 81)

Analysis of professional socialisation and patriarchal culture has traditionally relied upon feminist critique (e.g. Smith, 1978; Witz, 1992) Masculinity as an organisational issue is both ignored and taken for granted in the literature on management. As Collinson and Hearn (1994) assert, 'manager' and 'leader' equal man, unproblematically.

As a consequence of this invisible masculinity 'most organisations are saturated with masculine values' (Burton, 1991: 3, cited in Collinson and Hearn, 1994). Thus, as Dorothy Smith (1978) declared, 'women have been largely excluded from the work of producing the forms of thought and the images and symbols in which thought is expressed and ordered. There is a circle effect. Men attend to and treat as significant only what men say' (p.281). The result is that masculine aspects of professional culture are taken for granted, and socialisation into this context enables men but disables women.

Hence, the notion of the lifetime career and full-time work are part of a man's expectation, which is one of the reasons that unemployment and redundancy appears to be so destructive of men's mental health (Archer and Rhodes, 1993). Connected with this is the relationship between masculine identity and the role of the breadwinner/provider (Ehrenreich, 1983). Although there have been changes in emphasis over time, a crucial aspect of masculine identity is that a man should be able to support a wife and children. In order to do this, he has to be in paid employment, and if work is the key to his masculinity, work organisations are also likely to be a major site on which masculinity is rehearsed and confirmed.

Confirmation of masculinity occurs at a number of levels: the practical, discursive and the unconscious.

## Practical masculinity

This involves the process of simply 'being a man' in an unreflexive way, taking masculine ways of behaving and values for granted.[1] Such active confirmations of masculinity are unfamiliar to women, who are made to feel uncomfortable when subjected to 'laddish' behaviour. It frequently takes the form of sexual innuendo, and occurs in common rooms, during lunch time or at social gatherings after hours. It frequently occurs in formal meetings also, where jokes about sexual habits and *double entendres* are repeatedly employed to 'lighten the mood'. Many women find they either quietly exclude themselves from the repartee, take a full part, or disapprove at the risk of being censured for their lack of fun (see Cockburn, 1993).

Examples of this are common in medical education. Many young women find that in anatomy classes, it is considered acceptable to cut off a female breast and throw it in the waste bin, while penises and testicles are routinely treated with great reverence. Many who have made this observation are ridiculed by anatomy demonstrators (typically recently qualified junior doctors). This practice *per se* debases the female body, while the treatment of students' protests ensures that young women's public acknowledgement of this debasement is curtailed and may lead them to the recognition that they should be quiet about such matters.

Another germane example, which led to a female student making a successful complaint resulting in a minor disciplinary action, arose when a lecturer discussing obesity used the final ten minutes of the lecture to show slides of an extremely fat woman in a bikini, exhibiting a number of 'provocative' poses. When a female student complained that this was both gratuitous in that it contributed nothing to the lecture content and was sexist in that it devalued women, the male lecturer publicly humiliated her in front of more than 100 students by accusing her of being humourless.

This behaviour occurs in other professions as well. Cynthia Cockburn (1993) provides an example of a presentation given to a mixed-sex group of managers from a High Street retail company's computer division:

> The middle and senior staff of the Division had gone away together at company expense for a weekend's conference in a hotel. The occasion was intended to review the Division's work and build *esprit de corps*. The first morning's business opened with a presentation by a senior

manager. He had prepared a 'visual aid' in the form of a life-sized photograph of a bare-breasted model. In the photo she appeared leaning against a rock with a hole in it. In this space the senior manager had had superimposed a second photo, of the divisional director's face. He opened the talk as follows. 'We are lucky to have [the director] with us this morning. He's just risen from a sick bed. [pause for effect]. His secretary has flu'. This drew a laugh – not only from the audience but from the director – and from his secretary who was also present at the time. There followed other sexual allusions and jokes from this and subsequent speakers.

(Cockburn, 1993: 153–154)

This kind of behaviour, which appears to span the professions, emphasises woman as 'other'. They are either 'just' secretaries and 'justifiably' the objects of sexual innuendo, or they are kill-joys. What women are not, it seems, is part of the establishment, the foreground of professional organisations and culture. If they were, then this form of masculinity would be positioned as problematic.

## Discursive masculinity

Men, like women, actively construct their identities/subjectivities through reflexivity, developing their biographies over the course of time (see Chapter 2).

Career progression, as central to cultural notions of masculinity, becomes a key element in the construction of biography and subjectivity. Careers thus confer a meaning to subjective experiences of masculinity (see Collinson and Hearn, 1994).

Working with women who are in a subordinate position coheres with the operation of discursive consciousness and masculine subjectivity. Relationships with female juniors, secretaries, nurses or wives strengthen the conflation of masculinity and career. The traditional superordinate–subordinate pattern evolves from the time of a man's entry into the professional organisation to his achievement of senior status: son, brother, husband/boss. The brother–sister relationship is best accomplished while the man is still at the aspirational level where it remains possible, as with young children, to 'play' together. However, the young man expects to be chosen as the 'heir'. Working alongside or in a junior capacity, once he has outgrown the possibility that the woman is 'mother', is a deeply humiliating experience for some men.

In one example, a senior female manager in a health care service acted as mentor to a management trainee. She took an active interest in his career development and singled him out for involvement with some complex but high status projects, and ensured that where possible his role was made visible to the relevant members of the hierarchy. Like most people, his work was not always perfect, and on a few occasions she had to get him to rewrite reports, or was critical of the way he had handled a particular situation. He took the criticism seriously, and far from appearing resentful, he asked for as much feedback as she was willing to provide.

He left after completing the required training period, and three years later returned in a senior role, where the two of them were working at the same level, although she was the more experienced person and actively looking for promotion. At first, he tried to seek her support in the way he had before and was taken aback when she also came to him for advice and support. She had recognised their implicit equality, while he was still seeking the mother–son relationship. As the months passed however, he gradually distanced himself from her, and in fact, shortly before she left to take up a promoted post elsewhere, she realised that far from being her ally, he had made strong connections with colleagues she considered to be her enemies.

## Unconscious masculinity

Working with women as equals disrupts masculine subjectivity. That is not to say that all men are misogynist. One of the findings from my study of doctors, lecturers and medical students was the way that senior men's perspectives on gender discrimination were polarised. They were either deeply concerned and supportive of equal opportunities and angry about sexual harassment of women by men (for example: 'Sexual harassment can certainly have serious consequences for some individuals, and should be opposed whenever it occurs – especially in an academic establishment' (man in his forties) and 'Intentional harassment can harm (psychologically) individuals and if they are not secure, cause long-term problems' (man in his forties)) or they saw sexual harassment and the pursuit of equal opportunities as trivial or a joke (for instance: 'It's not the duty of medical educators' (man in his fifties); 'Sexual harassment is not a problem in my opinion' (man in his twenties); 'Life is too short and there are more pressing problems and needs of the student' (anonymous); and 'Does it exist?' (man in his thirties)).

Other men in the study were careless about equal opportunities issues, revealing underlying prejudice in the expression of their views. As one man said: 'Medical school starts with bias against males – by taking equal ratios of males and females. Many more males apply for medical school than females, and so the chance of a male being offered a place is less than a female' (anonymous male hospital consultant and honorary lecturer attached to a medical school). Or another: 'Sensible women will want to have a family and this is more compatible with some specialties than others' (anonymous male hospital consultant and honorary lecturer attached to a medical school).

It is difficult for men to experience women as equal or the same, and pressure to recognise women as equals and/or superiors caused by both policy and the characteristics of ambitious and capable women pre-cipitates anxiety, guilt and envy in the men.

## ENVY AND ANXIETY

Freud and subsequent psychoanalysts, as outlined in Chapter 3, theorised penis envy as a pathological female characteristic. Women wanted what they could never have – the penis and the phallus, the symbol of power. Other psychoanalytic writers, such as Erikson, have suggested that men may envy women their ability to bear children. What has not been suggested is that men might experience an equivalent to penis envy in their relationships with women.

Jane Ussher (1995) in her paper 'Masculinity as masquerade', discussed in Chapter 3, has suggested that men experience a fantasy or hope that their penis is, in fact, a phallus. She asserts that men are in fact condemned by the phallic illusion because the real organ and the real man rarely or never match up to the symbol. Ussher's paper focuses upon male sexual dysfunction and the representation of the penis/phallus in lesbian pornography. However, parallels may also be drawn in relation to professional culture. Men experience masculine subjectivity/identity through their relation to woman as 'other' and their superordinate relation to the women in their lives at various stages of their biographies. Even if they themselves do not achieve the professional accolade and success they desire, they see others like them doing so. This echoes Freud's idea of identification with the father or other men as resolution to the Oedipal crisis.

In patriarchal organisations, women on the whole are not in the higher echelons of power, so all is well. However, men are beginning to witness increased numbers of women entering their professional lives, and these women are refusing to go away. Many seem keen to achieve, some are managing to do so. Some senior men are beginning to take more notice of these women than they are of equivalent men. There are affirmative action programmes which may be seen to make things easier for women than for themselves. There is apparent turmoil and the possibility of seeing women with power. This seeming chaos and disturbance in the patriarchal order creates extreme anxiety and envy in many men and women. In the short term this may stimulate greater productivity through a sense of competitiveness, but if anxiety and envy are the basis of motivation, the final achievements will be pathological and damaging to health.

But what is envy in this context? Envy is a destructive and uncomfortable emotional state, and was brought to the fore in the psychoanalytic work of Melanie Klein. As Julia Segal writes, in her account of Klein's contribution to psychoanalysis, 'Envy is spoiling and damaging in nature, neatly expressed in "throwing shit" at someone or something' (Segal, 1992: 54).

Here I want to examine the role of envy in the creation of an organisational culture that is damaging to women and to men. In doing so I briefly examine the work of Melanie Klein and the object-relations school of psychoanalysis.

## Melanie Klein, anxiety and envy

Melanie Klein specialised in working with infants and young children. She began her career with Freud, but departed from his theories to develop her own controversial perspectives. The main source of contention between Freud and Klein was her perspective on the Oedipus complex and the development of the superego (see discussion of this in Chapter 3). In contrast to Freud, she believed that major psychic developments took place in the first six months of life. Klein argued that the first relationship an infant has is with the mother's breast, not as Freud believed with itself alone, or later, the mother as a whole person. This object, and the relationship the infant has with it influences all subsequent ones. This fantasy 'breast', however, was an object endowed with meaning that went beyond that of a mammary gland producing milk. Klein found that fantasies about the breast included the breast as a source of comfort, love, hope, babies, peace and serenity. Babies fantasised about taking this breast into themselves and fusing with it. There were, conversely, fantasies about being eaten by it, torn apart or threatened, of the breast being damaged or dangerous inside and outside of the baby. These primitive fantasies Klein hypothesised belonged to the *paranoid-schizoid position* (Segal, 1992: 41).

As the baby grows, it realises that the breast does not have a life of its own, but is part of the mother and not the baby herself. This development takes place under the influence of the more mature *depressive position* (Segal, 1992: 41).

The depressive position is not comfortable, and under stress the child or adult may attempt to get rid of the new awareness that it brings. The individual splits the object into the 'good' and the 'bad'. This creates what Klein called 'part-objects' as a defence against persecutory fantasies, which includes the defence mechanism of 'idealisation'. It may be illustrated thus:

> A small girl's own envy and jealousy of her mother is painful reality: in her attempts to get rid of this she creates Cinderella's envious step-mother, a persecutory fantasy. The fairy-godmother and Cinderella, as a helpless innocent victim, are both idealisations which then defend the girl from the phantasy woman.
>
> (Segal, 1992: 42)

## Anxiety

Where the paranoid-schizoid position deals in part-objects, the infant under the influence of the depressive position becomes much more aware of whole objects, in which characteristics felt to be loved and good co-exist with those felt to be bad and dangerous. At the same time the child (or adult) feels more integrated, whole and human, sharing good and bad characteristics and conflicts with others.

Anxiety, according to Klein, following Freud, relates to aggressive, destructive instincts (e.g. the 'death instinct'), which exist from the start of life in opposition to the 'life instinct'. The child has early fears about her own aggressive impulses and fears attacks from a vengeful mother/breast which the child has taken into her own body. This fear Klein called 'persecutory anxiety' which is part of the paranoid-schizoid position.

Klein distinguished this from anxiety in the depressive position in which the fears are for the safety of the mother/breast. This anxiety is qualitatively different from persecutory anxiety and more bearable.

Anxiety is important in Klein's theorising and clinical work because seeking the source of a present anxiety can bring relief. Anxiety can also prevent or motivate change. For instance, reflecting upon anxiety may lead to reorganising style of work, changing organisation or career. Under the pressure of persecutory anxieties, 'splitting', 'disintegration' and 'denial' take place, which prevent change and avoid facing external processes. Under the burden of depressive anxieties, integration and acceptance of reality may occur (Segal, 1992: 53).

## Envy

> Envy is the angry feeling that another person possesses and enjoys something desirable – the envious impulse being to take it away or to spoil it. Moreover, envy implies the subject's relation to one person only and goes back to the earliest exclusive relation with the mother. Jealousy is based on envy, but involves a relation to at least two people; it is mainly concerned with love that the subject feels is his due and has been taken away, or is in danger of being taken away, from him by his rival.
>
> (Klein, 1975: 181)

Envy originates from the paranoid-schizoid position and jealousy from the depressive. Klein believed that envy, arising in the earliest stage of infancy, was the source of many adult difficulties. Envy destroys pleasure in the self and others, so that the envious parts of the mind may prevent happiness, creativity and success for everyone (Segal, 1992: 54).

## Defences against anxiety and gender relations

Dividing feelings into good and bad, which enables children and adults to gain relief from internal conflicts, is called *splitting*. This process is often accompanied by *projection*, which involves locating the feelings in others than oneself. Thus unpleasant qualities such as slyness, dishonesty, stupidity and so on are seen only as the attributes of the other.

In relationships it may be possible for the other person, unconsciously, to experience the feelings that are being projected into them. This process is called *projective identification*. The state of mind whereby other people's feelings are experienced as one's own is called *countertransference*. Projective identification often leads to recipient's acting out the counter-transference derived from the projected feelings. These processes often occur in organisations under threat whereby managers might experience distress and depression projected by staff under notice of redundancy (Halton, 1994).

Projective identification as a defence against anxiety and envy in gender relations provides key insights into interpersonal life. This may be the case particularly in professions and organisations where women are increasing in number. Women entering business, management, academia or the traditional professions, even if they are not specifically ambitious, do not neatly fit the feminine stereotype, as I have argued.

This may precipitate a sense of chaos and threat to those in established roles.

In some contexts this perceived absence of feminine qualities in these women might be extremely distressing for the men they work alongside or who are being managed directly by them. Nursing, social work, psychotherapy, academia – particularly in the 'softer' subjects, certain aspects of the law (e.g. marital work) or medicine (e.g. public health medicine, family planning) – may be seen as areas which are more accessible to women, and therefore men's sense of masculinity and potency are under greater threat than say in finance or engineering.

The following example will illustrate what I mean. A well-qualified woman academic (Janet) was appointed as a lecturer to a university English Literature department. She had been an academic for years and published widely, although, like many academics experiencing a career log-jam, had not gained a promoted post. She moved institution to what was perceived as a more prestigious department, in order to effect a career move. Her male colleague (John), with a similar specialisation, who was to share the teaching of a course with her, seemed at interview to be pleasant, relaxed and welcoming. John had a respectable publishing record, but did not have Janet's high profile, which she had achieved through international interest in her work on women in literature. He, like her, was hoping for a promotion before too long, as they were both at the top of the lecturer pay scale. When she arrived to take up her post, however, she found him changed. He would not spare her the time for a chat or to show her the library, nor would he introduce her to anyone, despite her request to meet a few key people. This made her feel vulnerable and isolated, particularly because she was in a new town and her family had remained behind to sell their house. This feeling of isolation was made even worse when she set about the task of meeting people off her own bat, and they told her how pleasant John was and how pleased he had been at her appointment. She was perplexed.

As time passed, she became confident in her own networks, but it remained a problem not to have a comfortable working relationship with her closest colleague, particularly when their part of the English department came under threat of a move to a less suitable building, far away from the lecture theatres and library. She kept stressing to John that they could best fight the threat by working together and sharing information (something he had not done before). She noticed that under stress he would come to see her and talk. It would start with him saying he was worried about a certain development, and Janet would reciprocate with her attempt at empathy and analysis and expression of her own feeling. Were they going to manage a working relationship at last? The pattern began to emerge that following her sharing her anxieties with him, he would leave. She was left feeling anxious and even more isolated than before he came into the room, feeling as if she had misunderstood the politics or practicalities of the developing crisis over accommodation. Eventually she had a physical collapse following a panic attack. She noted that he avoided her for several weeks following her panic attack, while she coped and received adequate sympathy from others.

One day, a colleague with whom she had become friendly said to Janet how amazing it was that John had remained so relaxed all through the (now resolved) accommodation crisis. Janet suddenly realised what had been going on.

John, who valued his relaxed, friendly style, had been threatened by the arrival of the high-profile, hard-working and energetic Janet. She would move quickly and impatiently around the department, and within a few months of taking up the post had made some interesting and important friends at the university. This had made John particularly worried that she would gain the edge and get her promotion before him.

However, Janet was also insecure. John had played upon her isolation and vulnerability as a new person by not supporting her, and also on her need for social contacts and co-operation under the threat of the office move by enabling her to express fears which he saw were as strong as his own. Instead of enabling her to alleviate some of her anxieties as she had done for him, he would cut off and leave.

John, who despised manifestations of anxiety in others, was overwhelmed by his own internal persecutory anxiety which had its origins in unresolved situations from infancy and childhood. He therefore split it off and projected it into other people, so he was then able to see himself as ultra-relaxed and others as tense. In this case Janet was an ideal target for his projections. She was vulnerable and made anxious by (mainly) outside factors such as being new and having the threat of the office move crisis looming. He envied her abilities and high profile and the fact that she had gained attention from people who regarded him as pleasant but insignificant. By projecting his despised anxiety onto Janet, he was able to dismiss her in his own mind.

*He* could not cope otherwise with his anxiety or his envy. The more stressed *she* became, the more she accepted the countertransference, eventually becoming so anxious that she collapsed. Not until she realised what was happening could she observe his behaviour dispassionately.

John, unaware of her insight, continued to try and rekindle the anxieties and insecurities in Janet, but to no avail as she had both gained understanding of their relationship and the external crises had gone away. She had been reacting to outside threats initially, but through the process of projective identification had taken in John's anxiety (which was internal to him, although fuelled by Janet's arrival and by the accommodation issue).

Her anxiety was resolved, but his situation became more acute because he was unable to project onto Janet anymore. Even when he did get his promotion before she did, he did not feel released from his internal persecutors.

This example involved a woman and a man, but why is it generalisable to gender at work? Janet and John worked in a patriarchal context, and although John eventually was promoted and Janet was not, John was not a 'success' in his own eyes. His subject area was not traditionally masculine, and whereas other men in his field had moved up the hierarchy to management or built international reputations, constantly flying from one conference to another, he was 'just' a lecturer. Janet, on the other hand, was well known, and as a woman had achieved more than many other women by gaining a permanent post in a prestigious department. Also, as a woman,[2] she was used to being sociable and sharing with colleagues, especially under threat. She was also able to relate without difficulty to senior male colleagues. John found this difficult because it reinforced his junior status in relation to them. Janet had a sense of personal responsibility for the future welfare of their branch of literature in the department and university, and for those reasons she found it impossible to detach herself from the accommodation crisis issue, and in order to be effective she knew she needed John's co-operation. John would have been aware of that need and expectation. His feelings about Janet overshadowed his concern and sense of responsibility towards his work. He wanted to exploit and destroy her because her presence humiliated him, as did the presence of other successful women. What made Janet special, however, was her comparability – age, career stage and subject area. Given her starting point he knew that she was likely to outstrip him, and that this would be a public and unbearable humiliation.

This pattern, whereby the woman is better qualified than the man, is likely to become increasingly common. It echoes the cliché that a woman has to be twice as good as a man to achieve the same recognition, but the point here is that there are double problems for women as men realise this and see female colleagues as a threat.

In the following chapter, I outline the way that these unconscious processes and defence mechanisms occur on an institution-wide basis.

## CONCLUSIONS

Understanding gender relations at work cannot be achieved through traditional, 'objective' means alone. Psychometric measurement and the facts and figures which represent the changing structures of organisations and professional groups do provide important clues about trends. For instance, without statistics on the numbers of women in senior management posts, the influence on organisations of equal opportunities policies, wider demographic and educational trends would not be available. Surveys may also provide strong evidence of the existence, scope, location and style of, for example, sexual harassment. However, quantification is only half the story. Women and men engage in power politics in conscious and unconscious ways, on both a grand and small scale. Patriarchal organisations value men and patriarchy more than they value women and their accomplishments. Many women are not only being forced to fail, but also are suffering ill health as a consequence. Through employing a feminist analysis of organisational culture, it is possible to construct and deconstruct biographies to reveal power struggles that are pervasive and damaging to equality which ultimately disclose more about power and gender politics than do statistics.

## NOTES

1  I am not implying any biological aspect, but referring to the ideas developed in Chapter 2.
2  This is not intended to be a crude gender stereotype, but relates to issues raised earlier in this chapter which indicate that although women have no innate social propensity, nevertheless for a variety of structural and historical reasons they have different interactional styles and expectations.

# Chapter 5

# In the shadow of the glass ceiling

## INTRODUCTION

Many women are blocked in their attempts to gain access to the higher reaches of public and professional life. They remain clustered in positions that fail to make full use of their qualifications and abilities. Over 70% of women work in lower-level clerical and service sector jobs; over 40% of women work in jobs where they have no male colleagues For too many there is a glass ceiling over their aspirations – it allows them to see where they might go, but stops them getting there. In any given occupation and in any given public position, the higher the rank, prestige or power, the smaller the proportion of women.
(Hansard Society Commission, 1990: 15)

Much has been written about the glass ceiling in recent years (Hansard Society Commission, 1990; Davidson and Cooper, 1992; Flanders, 1994). Women do break through and achieve senior positions, but the more senior a woman becomes, the more isolated she is from other women. The issues here are the psychological costs of success and how far the fact of some women's success has the potential to break the glass ceiling for others.

In this chapter I progress from an analysis of the individual and interpersonal aspects of gender at work, to distinguish the impact on successful women of the group and organisational practices which subordinate women in professional life. Despite the success of some, women's achievement continues to take place in the patriarchal context, which most readily displays male success and female failure. This potentially restricts the way women and others realise and explain their achievements, as well as the means by which they negotiate their relationships in the context of their biographies and within patriarchal culture.

At the end of Chapter 4, I outlined the threats to men and patriarchal culture imposed by women's rise up organisational hierarchies. Here I want to explore the implications of male success for *women's experiences*, particularly their management of self-esteem, relationships with other women, assessment of their own career potential and their emotional and mental health.

To effect this I focus, first, on how far the patriarchal organisational structures of professions constrain the lives of the women within them; second, on the psychological consequences of this; and third, I identify the factors that hinder change and those which encourage it.

## ORGANISATIONAL STRUCTURES AND PROFESSIONAL WOMEN'S LIVES

> Few in 1982 . . . let alone ten years on . . . would have said that this expectation of equality, either at work or at home, had been met.
>
> (Apter, 1993: 2).

The figures outlined in the introduction to this book provide clear evidence that male bastions of power in the professions and in the domestic sphere have remained firmly in place. These dual areas of subordination doubly disadvantage professional women striving for and achieving success in senior posts.

These figures are further supported by evidence from The Hansard Society Commissions (1990) report *Women at the Top*, which demonstrates a serious under-representation of women in all positions of social, professional and political influence. At 6.3 per cent, the UK parliament has the lowest proportion of female MPs in Western Europe. Similarly, in the House of Lords only 13 per cent of life peers are women, although the Commission suggest that 'even this is better than the dismal representation of women in the Commons' (p. 4). In public office, female appointments remain low despite active measures to recruit women to government posts. Less than one-fifth of all honours go to women. The judiciary, the Civil Service, the legal profession, senior management, company boardroom directors, academia, the media and trade unions all have few women in senior influential positions.

### What do these patterns reveal?

It is clear that 'unofficial' discrimination has taken place over a number of years. In the medical profession for example, from 40–50 per cent of medical school entrants have been women for nearly twenty years, but the proportion represented at the higher echelons of clinical practice suggests that there must be insurmountable barriers (Department of Health, 1991–2).

Women are scarcely found in upper management in the newspaper and magazine world, despite the preponderance of women readers, especially of magazines (Hansard Society Commission, 1990). Similarly, the upper echelons of television demonstrate a marked absence of women in influential roles. In publishing in the UK, 75 per cent of employees in editorial departments are women, but few get to the ranks above editor. Men are more than twice as likely to become managers in publishing (see Hansard Society Commission, 1990).

The fact that initiatives to change this state of affairs (such as equal opportunities programmes of various kinds: e.g. Opportunity 2000 in the UK National Health Service, WIST (Women in Surgical Training) and part-time training programmes set up by the Royal College of Obstetricians and Gynaecologists) have met with only limited success, further serves to indicate the strength of institutionalised prejudice.

Constraints on women's lives in patriarchal organisations are characterised by various forms of discrimination which take an invisible toll on their health (emotional and physical). Women are still the 'other' or marginal to the main organisational objectives, even when successful. Women who are successful are isolated from other women by definition.

## Processes of discrimination

Widespread discrimination still occurs and has consequences for all women and men. Women who break through the traditional career barriers are no less subject to the processes than those who do not.

There are three kinds of discriminatory processes which are increasingly well documented and which keep the patriarchal structures in place. These are the *overt* structural barriers such as lack of child-care facilities, lack of role models or mentors for women; the *covert* barriers such as prejudiced attitudes, beliefs and male-defined exclusionary behaviour; and the *unconscious* psychological impact of patriarchal organisations on women's motivation, self-esteem and the reflexive relationship between biographical context and knowledge. This is often hidden from women themselves in that the impact of the patriarchal seeps into the discourses women employ to achieve a reflexive self-evaluation.

### Overt structural barriers to women's careers: motherhood

> the amount of support women receive from their partners is limited . . . traditional role models are usually maintained.
>
> (Simpson, 1991: 120)

Overt structural barriers are established and integral to organisational arrangements, and are thus the most visible. For example, women are still charged with domestic and child-care responsibilities to a far greater extent than men (Apter, 1993). Few organisations have day-care facilities, and long working hours discriminate against those with primary child-care responsibilities. The child-blind organisational context supports the habit of early morning and evening meetings, which eat into 'out of hours' and domestic time, potentially making attendance difficult for women, or makes their lack of attendance embarrassing.

As Carolyn Kagan and Sue Lewis (1990a) argue in their account of working as academic psychologists:

> No allowances have been made because we have families, and no formal or informal offers of reorganising responsibilities or timetables have been forthcoming. It is not only women who have had families. However, all the men with families have had wives who stopped working for various lengths of time when their children were born.
>
> (1990a: 21)

The disproportionate relationship between gender and domestic/child-care responsibility also disadvantages women because they cannot expect to have their meals cooked and children cared for ready for their return from work. As White et al. (1992) observe from their summary of the literature, even full-time career women perform the overwhelming majority of domestic and child-care tasks (p. 189). Successful women, as with men, have to give up time with their children for the sake of their careers, but unlike men, women's role in relation to parenting is constantly being discussed in the media and at various interpersonal levels. Therefore, even if a woman has chosen to be child-free or employ professional full-time child care, she is in constant danger of reproach, or having to justify her choice, from colleagues, friends and family.

**Mentors**

Another observable barrier to women's achievement has been the lack of female role models and mentors. Studies have shown that same-sex mentors are beneficial, which puts women at a disadvantage because of limited choice (Richey et al., 1988). White and colleagues (1992) have indicated in their 'profile' of the successful career woman that she is likely to have identified an individual who has been influential in her career and acted to raise confidence in her own abilities. They found that mentors also gave practical help, but did not particularly act as role models. The modest number of senior female figures in commerce, industry and the professions suggests that if a woman has a mentor, it is likely to be a man. While male mentors might be effective in the medium term, there are problems with long-term relationships between senior men and up-and-coming women. Issues of sexuality and power are likely to inhibit the quality of the relationship (see Chapter 6 for a fuller discussion).

In order to overcome the lack of mentors, especially for women and other minority groups, some formal mentoring schemes are being introduced. There are, however, interesting differences between formal mentoring schemes and informal mentoring.

One clinical psychology training scheme, for example, organises graduate trainees to meet with allocated mentors at least three times a year during the three years of their professional training. The aim is to consider clinical issues and to enable the trainee to discuss their anxieties and the pleasures they achieve from their work. These include practical, clinical, ethical, career and interpersonal work-related issues, but not academic work. This relationship continues for the first year following the completion of the training (and thus is four years in total). The mentor is normally a trained and experienced clinical psychologist, and generally there is no element of personal choice in the relationship. This scheme has yet to be evaluated formally, but the feedback is generally positive in that clinical psychology trainees feel they have gained support and knowledge through these relationships. However, such a scheme potentially lacks the emotional ties which bind the partners who choose each other.

One example, illustrative of how choice in the mentoring relationship can result in a long-term, mutually beneficial commitment was an effective informal association among a group of three male academics. Professor A, in his late fifties when the relationship started, was a pro-vice chancellor,[1] and had taken an interest in the career of Professor B, recently appointed to a chair in the same subject area, supported by Professor A. Dr C, appointed to Professor B's department, was included in their social round, and Professor B brought him to the attention of Professor A. When a new Chair was created, four years after Dr C's appointment, Professor A, who had had several opportunities to meet and encourage Dr C, urged him to apply. Professor B helped Dr C to polish up his CV, and Professor A was a member of the board who duly appointed Dr C to the chair.

There is no sense in which I am suggesting that Dr C was not an ideal and probably even the best candidate for the post. What is important to note is the process through which he was groomed and encouraged. All three members of this network took the fact of their relationships for granted. They all benefited from supporting each other, even though all three were at different career stages. The older men achieved a stake in the future, but were still active on committees to which eventually all three were involved and offered mutual support – in public and in private.

This informal model is more effective in terms of career advancement and motivation than any formal system could be. The system cannot work for women in the same way because there is not the long-term continuity or the number of women to make this possible, and neither is there a tradition of such practice. It is difficult for cross-sex, long-term relationships to work effectively because they are likely to give rise to sexual gossip and speculation (Hearn and Parkin, 1987; Davidson and Cooper, 1992; see also Chapter 6).

## Overtly sexist attitudes

Blatant sex discrimination includes those discriminatory actions directed against women that are quite obvious to most observers and are highly visible.
(Benokraitis and Feagin, 1995: 59)

Overtly sexist attitudes range from sexist remarks and jokes in meetings or public spaces at work, to violent and abusive behaviour from sexual harassment to rape (Anderson et al., 1993). These actions have negative implications for women at all levels of the organisation. Seniority is no barrier to sexism.

Anti-women remarks and behaviours occur in formal situations such as committee meetings, appointment or promotion boards. Sexist remarks in general make it difficult for women committee members. Should they object every time something sexist is said or wait until there are potentially serious consequences that may influence a promotion or appointment panel? They risk making dangerous and permanent enemies, being further labelled as outsiders, accused of lack of humour and being excluded from such panels in future because they cause trouble.

A woman being assessed by an appointment panel is still at risk of being asked questions about her domestic commitments or, if she is unmarried, facing questions or innuendo about her sexuality.

However, it is not only men who hold sexist attitudes. One survey of accountants, civil engineers, surveyors, bankers, lawyers, architects, computer managers and insurers in the UK (MORI, 1994) made it clear that 'Women would rather work with men than with other women . . . . Four times as many professional women would prefer to be surrounded by men at work, than by women' (MORI, 1994: 7). Also, around 25 per cent of the women surveyed said they would prefer a male to a female boss, despite reported experiences of discrimination. Only 4 per cent of men said they wanted a female boss, which suggests that female bosses have poor quality day-to-day relationships at work if most colleagues view them so disapprovingly.

## Sexual harassment

Sexual harassment, which includes anything from drawing attention to a woman's body, causing embarrassment and demanding sexual favours, is a powerful discriminatory factor and may occur to women at any stage of their career. The remarks may be apparently approving of a woman's body, as is frequently the case with junior staff and students. For older, more senior women, it is more likely to be derogatory. According to numerous workplace surveys, this male behaviour seems commonplace – I found that around 25 per cent of medical students reported being aware of sexual harassment taking place at university (Nicolson and Welsh, 1992). This corresponded to other university surveys (e.g. Sheffield University Student Union, 1992). (See Chapter 6 for more details and discussion of sexual harassment.) The consequences of unchallenged sexual harassment are to poison the organisational culture, both in the long term and on a daily basis (see below in this chapter and Chapter 6).

## Backlash: covert barriers to women's success: complaining

Policies to combat overt sexism are limited in their effectiveness as they require the victim to report the perpetrator's behaviour. One example of this is the NHS action plan for implementation and monitoring of Opportunity 2000. The intent, that is to combat sexist behaviour, is clear, but sanctions for transgression stated in the documentation are obscure. A brief reference to complaints procedures is as follows:

> Any woman who wants to complain about not being treated fairly under these procedures should put her complaints in writing to her general manager/chief executive with a copy to the non-executive director with specific responsibility for women's issues.
>
> (NHS Management Executive, 1992: 5)

This blanket procedure, intended to apply to women doctors as well as other health service employers, is bizarre. There is an abundance of anecdotal and an increase in empirical research based data to suggest that this individualistic response is problematic and is unlikely to happen, except in severe cases, where a person's life becomes intolerable[2] (Aitkenhead and Liff, 1990). Women making complaints of sexual harassment and discrimination are routinely humiliated and their working environment is often hostile.

While it seems impossible for effective complaints to be made against senior men, complaints against senior women are numerous and well publicised. Such complaints have themselves been perceived as a form of discrimination. Wendy Savage, a senior lecturer and honorary consultant in obstetrics and gynaecology was suspended during the mid 1980s for professional misconduct (Savage, 1986).[3] Her subsequent analysis of events leading up to and following this affair made explicit the role of gender–power relations in the clinical establishment. Savage attributed her suspension and criticisms made of her clinical practice directly to the patriarchal structure of medicine and its operation within her speciality of obstetrics and gynaecology in particular, as well as inherent misogyny operating on a personal level in her health authority. Her account detailed discriminatory processes at several levels: the interpersonal, the organisational and the cultural. There seemed no individual, or structure within the hospital, health authority or Royal College, that was not inherently biased in favour of the male dominated status quo. Thus her defence was supported largely by friends, lawyers and patients rather than from within the obstetrics and gynaecology hierarchy (Savage, 1986).

## Patriarchal culture

The patriarchal culture in all professions and business organisations is endemic. Women are invisible, and what they do is second-rate compared with what men do. Covert barriers to women's career progression represent the 'backlash' to the perceived threat of the rise of women's power in organisations.

The patriarchal culture of professional organisations is, paradoxically, both clearly visible yet hidden during the socialisation processes that occur when young women and men enter the system.

At medical school, for example, where socialisation begins as an undergraduate, the deep-rooted value system in relation to who is going to be a successful (as opposed to 'good') doctor is transmitted to medical students of both sexes: e.g. that men make better hospital consultants and women make better general practitioners (Nicolson and Welsh, 1992).

In clinical psychology, the path to qualification and promotion is more complex: acceptance on the postgraduate training course is dependent upon a good first degree result (and sometimes a PhD) and a selection interview. Because up to 90 per cent of psychology undergraduates are women (Morris et al., 1990), there is hidden pressure to reduce the proportion of women at each of these stages to enable men to achieve places on the clinical psychology courses. Thus it is more difficult for women to get to the first rung of the ladder. Women doctors have an advantage because they do not have to compete to get to this stage, and there are only 50 per cent at the start of the course, so fear of them appears to be not so great, but it is increasing.

One example of covert discrimination reported by Wendy Savage was The Royal College of Obstetricians and Gynaecologists, where male members are invited to join clubs for which membership is limited to selected men alone and women seem unable or unwilling to contest this, either by seeking membership or forming parallel associations.

> Excluded from the cosy male get-togethers where, it is rumoured, all the consultant posts are 'fixed', women have formed their own club but it does not seem to be an effective pressure group for women, either as obstetricians or as patients. The incongruity of a specialty devoted to women being almost totally controlled by men has always struck me forcefully.
>
> (Savage, 1986: 59)

The level at which policy and practice are organised and the speciality is regulated has an effect that penetrates postgraduate medical education and cannot be eradicated by the introduction of part-time training posts and the acceptance of career breaks.

Women, it seems, are evaluated on criteria other than those used to evaluate men. There are recent examples where this is blatantly clear. For example, Helena Daly was sacked from a consultant post in 1993 for 'personal misconduct' when it was alleged she had been rude to secretaries and nurses. A letter in the *British Medical Journal*, on behalf of the Medical Women's Federation in support of her, made it clear that she had been judged as a *woman* rather than a doctor and that this was a relatively common occurrence.

These echo issues that social scientists have known about for many years, and yet they are as alive today as ever. It is that there is a mismatch between the image of the valued, successful senior professional and the image of the 'normal' woman (cf. Broverman et al., 1970). Dorothy Smith (1978) argued twenty years ago that:

> Men attend to and treat as significant only what men say. The circle of men whose writing and talk was significant to each other extends backwards in time as far as our records reach. What men were doing

was relevant to men, was written by men about men for men. Men listened and listen to what one another said.

(Smith, 1978: 281).

A few years before, it had been made quite clear that women in the professions are excluded *because they are not men*. Women have a 'servant' image, and the origin of this is 'the assumption that women innately, instinctively, or hormonally are adept at nurturing, sacrificing, and caring for others' (Prather, 1971: 17). Further, as a servant, 'American society implies women are better qualified than men for nurturant occupations, which are usually paid less and are of lower status than other professions .... [E]mployers can feel justified ... avoiding promoting women into positions of leadership'(Prather, 1971: 17).

So the identification and challenging of patriarchal bias is not new, yet it is persistent and underpins the formal processes through which promotions are achieved and power is distributed. However, it appears that the more patriarchy is challenged, the more energy is given to the backlash (Faludi, 1992).

## Old boy networks

What makes those in power so aware of women, especially powerful women, as different from themselves? Men, groomed for power, often find themselves in formal and informal decision-making contexts with men they have known at school, university or in previous career posts. Loyalty to such peers is frequently referred to as the 'old boy network' and reinforced through membership of formal or informal groups such as elite golf clubs, membership of gentleman's clubs, after hours drinking, rugby clubs and similar activities from which women are either by definition excluded, such as the Masons, or made to feel uncomfortable by being there, such as all-male, after hours social events (Davidson and Cooper, 1992: Flanders, 1994; Benokraitis and Feagin, 1995). As one woman in Davidson and Cooper's study said:

I felt very isolated. They would all go to all-male clubs at lunch time and that, of course, is where a lot of the real business goes on. Of course, I was therefore totally excluded from that. That was a big source of prejudice by them. It would have been much easier for me if there had been another woman in my position.

(Davidson and Cooper, 1992: 88)

Such networks however, are not only about excluding non-members, but are concerned with the socialisation of younger professionals and information giving. Women, therefore, are unable to learn ways of behaving. The 'old boy network' is the continuation of the socialisation into masculinity discussed in Chapter 4 and, as argued in that chapter, masculinity is equivalent to senior management behaviour. It has thus been estimated that over 50 per cent of all jobs in management came through personal contacts of these kinds (Davidson and Cooper, 1992: 88). This reinforces the notion that the senior woman has further to climb to reach the top than her male peers.

## Patronage

The issue of patronage is closely linked to 'old boy networks', as well as to mentoring, in that senior men will often choose to assist the career of someone similar to themselves or to the people they admire. Patronage is overt in the medical profession, and there are several examples in academic life when a postgraduate student of the professor obtains an academic post in that department despite strong competition from outside. The British Medical Association has expressed concern about this system, aware of the way minority groups (i.e. those not reflected among the current senior echelons of the profession) are disadvantaged.

> patrons will relate best to those who follow their own image . . . . [T]his means that already disadvantaged groups such as women, overseas doctors and doctors of ethnic minority origin, are least likely to benefit from the system, even though they are in most need of support.
>
> (BMA, 1993: 1)

Wendy Savage, well aware of the issues of patronage and reproduction of values through recruitment, cites examples from decision-making processes about appointments. In one case, a male professor

> weighed in with a vote for 'the chap we know'. It was then that one of the panel mounted an amazing attack on the Australian woman, repeating gossip that she was a difficult woman to work with, continuing innuendo about her personal life which it would be wrong to repeat. I was disgusted by this behaviour and so angry that I could hardly express my disapproval. I left the room abruptly.
>
> (Savage, 1986: 24)

Many women who move up the career ladder are rejected, often under similar circumstances. They themselves, like Savage, might wish to publicise the behaviour of the senior men who actively and blatantly discriminate. However, it appears that far from assisting change, such publicity reduces other women's motivation (Benokraitis and Feagin, 1995).

## Bad behaviour?

But is anger and disapproval the way to tackle patronage or any other displays of prejudice that comprise the glass ceiling? The cost to women for expressing such unfeminine behaviour may be high. Women have to cope with a dual assessment: as professionals in competition with men, and as female professionals. As the latter, they have to be better than men professionally, and feminine both socially and professionally. It is a crucial dilemma.

It can be no coincidence that apart from Wendy Savage and Helena Daly, mentioned above, well publicised professional and personal misconduct cases in the medical profession (such as that of Marietta Higgs or Carole Starkey) have women at their centre, and part of the case against them is that colleagues were 'afraid' to tell them that their practices appeared to be inadequate (see Nicolson, 1993b), implying that they were neither good doctors nor good women. In these cases their professional colleagues fail either to train, correct or socialise these women, which left them exposed.

Does this mean that women really are difficult to work with and will not respond to criticism, or are there organisational factors which expose the mistakes of women rather than those of men?

> The bad behaviour of some doctors is accepted as the norm in a stressful environment. It may even be rewarded with respect and sometimes affection. How different the response if that doctor is a woman.
>
> (Markham, 1993: 686)

The problem for women is that they are almost exclusively isolated from other women when they reach senior positions. Although some may welcome this (MORI, 1994), it can lead to an unwillingness to support, and prejudice against, other women. This 'female misogyny' arises because of the complex way that patriarchal culture is embedded in our perceptions of organisational life. Women frequently use time and energy in their early careers discovering the exclusionary force of patriarchal culture. They once, perhaps, believed themselves to be the exceptions to the stereotypical woman they so despised (Williams and Giles, 1978). However, there is little comfort in being the Queen Bee, when the wolves are baying for the blood of a scapegoat. It is the woman who is dispensable.

## UNCONSCIOUS BARRIERS: IDENTIFYING THE BOUNDARIES

How far are members of organisations aware of the implications of their own behaviour? The young female professional or manager attending a board meeting for the first time only experiences her own strangeness and terror with the situation. She is noticeable in the minority as a woman; the men know each other and are like each other; men are familiar with the routine and assist newcomers. How can she know why some board members fear her presence? She sees herself as new and inexperienced. Some of them know from her qualifications and background and that she is on the 'fast track'. They may feel unable to welcome her as she represents a threat. Thus they behave as if she is invisible and a burden. But why is she perceived as such a threat? There is no evidence that women are going to take over companies or professional groups in any large numbers.

The male head of a division finds it difficult to cope when he knows that the new female recruit is better qualified for *his* job than he is himself. As time passes she wonders what more she has to do to get his attention and praise. He is terrified that his incompetencies will be exposed and does what he (legitimately) can to hinder her finding out, and thus obstructs her progress.

In Chapter 4 I introduced the concepts of envy and anxiety as applied to men and women working in organisations. There, I suggested that instead of taking the traditional Freudian framework whereby women (unconsciously) envied men their power and success (i.e. envied their having a penis), it was increasingly the case that some men (unconsciously) envied women their skills and achievements. This was made more acute by the wider interest taken by feminist activists and academics, management scientists and politicians in women's progress. Here, I want to examine these aspects of the unconscious as they relate to organisational processes.

### The unconscious at work

Just as individuals operate defence mechanisms to protect themselves against anxiety, so do groups and organisations (Freud, 1921; Jaques, 1955; Bion, 1961; DeBoard, 1978).

Like individuals, institutions develop defences against difficult emotions which are too threatening or too painful to acknowledge. These emotions may be a response to external threats such as government policy or social change. They may arise from internal conflicts between management and employees or between groups and departments in competition for resources.

(Halton, 1994: 12)

In organisations, the unconscious operates at the level of the individual and the group/organisation itself. Unconscious processes are sources of energy, creativity and motivation at both of these levels, but unconscious defences against the overwhelming feelings of anxiety and envy frequently block energy which may result in poor emotional and/or physical health for all.

The implementation of equal opportunities policies, or the appointment of a female senior executive, may arouse group emotional responses that appear to have no basis in the changes that the policy or the appointment has actually precipitated. The large-scale defection of Church of England clergy to the Roman Catholic Church over the recognition of women priests was an example of this. Major anxieties were aroused by their fear of women having equal power and opportunities in the Church, but the Bible, God and personal conscience issues were produced as reasons for these defections. This process was really a large-scale denial of inherent misogyny in the organisation and those who ran it.

Organisations which comprise an increasing number of aspiring junior and middle ranking women are at crisis point. Men and women appear to have extensive fantasies and fears about changes that female management might bring that will increase the problems in their daily working lives and in their sense of subjectivity/identity.

**Men's fantasies and fears**

Accounts of men's concerns about women entering the higher echelons of their organisations and professions are (stereo)typically couched in 'logic'. Hence the infamous paper by Crawford (1989) about the state of the profession of clinical psychology in the UK, written at the time a major review was being carried out:

Almost all current trainees are female. The trend towards an increasingly female intake was first commented on in an article by Humphrey and Haward (1981) in which they said, 'if this trend were to continue there may well be cause for concern'. The trend has indeed continued and I believe there is cause for concern. First, there is the practical problem of a nearly all-female profession providing services for men. If the situation were reversed I am sure there would be numerous letters of complaint from women and quite rightly so. However, the problems of a female dominated profession are not just the mirror image of a male-dominated one. Whilst the BPS adheres to a non-sexist policy, the world at large is not necessarily so enlightened. National pay rates for women are significantly below those for men. Predominantly the female professions are lower in status and pay than predominantly male professions. Compare a nurse, teacher or occupational therapist with a surgeon, accountant or barrister.

As pay and status in clinical psychology have fallen, so men are no longer being attracted into the profession but as the profession becomes increasingly all female, so it will become harder to persuade general managers, mostly male, to improve pay and status: a downward spiral of a declining profession.

(Crawford, 1989: 30)

In fact Crawford's overt fears were unfounded. Clinical psychologists' salary scales were upgraded to the satisfaction of those within the profession. Women and men continue to enter the profession and compete for the senior and top positions, which are still mainly held by men. However, this is by no means exclusively so, and the trend towards women in powerful positions in clinical psychology is likely to continue.

What is interesting in this extract is the misogyny and anxiety couched in concern for standards. First, the writer, it seems, believes in equality but is anxious that the 'outside world' of managers and other policy-makers is not so enlightened, and thus salaries might fall compared to other groups. Second, there is the fear that a male patient might have to receive clinical treatment from a female psychologist. And third, there is the unstated fear that women might be promoted over the heads of men.

The denied anxiety in these 'logical' male fantasies seems to be about the subordination of men: that subordinated men are less than men – they have experienced the ultimate catastrophe: (metaphorical) castration. As in childhood, this anxiety is too much to bear and men need to find a variety of ways to defend themselves against this anxiety.

## The psychological consequences of barriers to women's careers

Some institutional defences are healthy, in the sense that they enable the staff to cope with stress and develop through their work in the organisations. But some institutional defences, like some individual defences, can obstruct contact with reality and in this way damage the staff and hinder the organisation in fulfilling its tasks and in adapting to changing circumstances. Central among these defences is *denial*, which involves pushing certain thoughts, feelings and experiences out of conscious awareness because they have become too anxiety provoking.

(Halton, 1994: 12)

Barriers to women's career progress, essentially conscious and deliberate on the part of *some* men, go largely unnoticed because they are about maintaining the status quo. However, they *do* have an unconscious negative influence on women, which reduces their motivation and has a derogatory influence on self-esteem.

Some women early in their careers *might* see sexist behaviour as a challenge or believe that some women specifically attract such comments and behaviours, but they themselves are the exceptions (as with the medical students discussed in Chapter 2). However, most women will come eventually to realise the constraints of patriarchy on their own careers as they make attempts to move up the hierarchy.

## CONCLUSIONS

Professional life, particularly for senior women in a patriarchal context, is stressful. Professional actions and decisions require expert knowledge and skilful execution, and thus daily life is characterised by a sense of responsibility which is likely at times to give rise to anxiety (see DeBoard, 1978). Men, particularly those who perceive threats from women or an individual woman, are also in danger of being overwhelmed.

Women witness the ease with which ordinary men achieve what they themselves are struggling to reach, and this brings about envious reactions, particularly in the isolated and battle weary. Men in senior positions watch better qualified, highly motivated women climbing the ladder towards them with unmitigated terror.

## NOTES

1   A senior academic/administrative post. Pro-vice chancellors chair policy and resources committees and normally take part with the vice-chancellor in all key policy decisions.
2   This is similar to Bruno Bettelheim's observation in *The Informed Heart* (1979) that victims will only fight their oppressors when they intuitively feel there is nothing left to lose. When a person still feels they have career potential, they are likely to try to carry on despite the sexual harassment.
3   She was cleared of all charges by the inquiry.

# Chapter 6

# Sexuality, power and organisation

## INTRODUCTION

> [men] dominate the sexual and emotional agenda, most profoundly by not
> perceiving they have one and that the sexual agenda is that of women.
>
> (Parkin, 1993: 168)

Male sexuality underlies the patriarchal culture of professional and
organisational life. 'Women work as "women"' (MacKinnon, 1979: 9),
and as such they are positioned as objects of male desire (see Chapter 3).
The fact of gender at work, and the ways in which gender–power relations
are conducted within patriarchal cultures overall, makes sexuality a
crucial component of these power relations.

In this chapter I re-examine the way in which the construction of
femininity and masculinity 'sexes' organisational life and, in so doing,
exacerbates the subordination of women to male desire.

I am thus concerned with identifying the processes whereby men and
patriarchy exert power over women through both verbal and physical
sexual harassment, while imposing constraints on women's *own* sexual
desire and behaviour in the context of the sexed organisational hierarchy.
While ambitious and influential men may gain credibility from visible
sexual activity and position themselves as active, potent and creative,
professional women are assumed to have to choose between being the
bimbo/whore or the asexual, serious professional woman. It is no
coincidence that sexual relations at work directly resemble sexual
relations outside.

This arrangement, which conflates power, influence and sexuality, not
only privileges men and heterosexuality, but devalues women's working
experiences through the threat or reality of harassment and forfeiture of
their own sexuality and expressions of desire.

## CONSTRUCTING SEXUALITY AT WORK

whilst men were positioned as the active driving force, the 'naturally' sexual beings, women were seen to be playing a key role in arousing male desire. Women's sexuality was therefore both fatal and flawed – paradoxically framed either as absent, within the archetype of the asexual pure Madonna, or as the all-encompassing and dangerously omnipotent, an image represented most clearly by the witch or the whore.

(Ussher, 1993: 10–11)

Men have power in organisations and professional life, while women are in subordinate positions (see Chapter 5). Women, as subordinates and the objects of male desire, are often seen by men as one of the 'benefits' of their position. The master–servant relationship whereby the woman/secretary will make coffee, buy cigarettes or cater to the male boss's emotional or sexual needs is the subject of myth, fiction and reality. Many men frequently behave as if women in these subordinate roles in the office are also available sexually (MacKinnon, 1979; Morris, 1994). They might likewise assume that other men see women in that way.

The sexual exploitation of women by men occurs when men have direct power over women's conditions of work and their hiring and firing – as in the case of secretaries, shop floor factory workers, waitresses and domestic staff. These workers tend to have little power, in that their lack of formal qualifications and skill makes them easily replaceable.

As MacKinnon depicts :

In such jobs a woman is employed as a woman. She is also, apparently, treated like a woman, with one aspect of this being specifically sexual. Specifically, if part of the reason a woman is hired is to be pleasing to the male boss, whose notion of a qualified worker merges with a sexist notion of the proper role of women, it is hardly surprising that sexual intimacy, forced when necessary, would be considered part of her duties and his privileges.

(MacKinnon, 1979: 18)

However, it is not only 'blue collar' men who enjoy these luxuries. As Wolf (1991) observes, the rules which governed employment in what had been specifically 'display professions', such as fashion modelling, actresses, night-club hostesses and so on, where beauty had been a requirement, appear to have been extended. 'What is happening today is that all the professions into which women are making strides are being rapidly reclassified – *so far as the women are concerned* – as display professions' (Wolf, 1991: 27, original emphasis). Thus female bank managers, lawyers and head teachers of schools all have to look both powerful and sexy. The appearance of Marcia Clark, the female prosecution lawyer in the O.J. Simpson murder trial, which was televised throughout the world, has been the subject of direct discussion. Television programmes, news and comment in the media have focused on the length of her skirts and manner of clothing. This reached a peak when she changed her hairstyle. Why should this be the case? Her legal skills, clearly on display, were deemed by the media to be less relevant to the proceedings than her sexual appeal. Her colleagues and the defence lawyers (mostly men) were discussed in a variety of ways, but it was only with her that appearance was on the agenda. Women as professionals have to tread a tightrope between visibility and invisibility *because of this positioning as sexual*, and dress style, gestures and language are part of this (Sheppard, 1989).

Some occupations for women are seen as almost equivalent to mistress/sex-object/whore. Secretaries, waitresses and nurses in particular, have traditionally been positioned in this way by the men who work in a superordinate rank. MacKinnon quotes an example of one secretarial college attempting to help their graduates ensure employment: 'The advice was to "sell" themselves. To do this they are made into a "pretty package"' (MacKinnon, 1979: 21).

One of the most blatant contexts for women being seen as sex objects by men, while they are seeing themselves as potential professionals, is the university (Butler and Landells, 1995). There, some male academics/ lecturers appear to judge all female students by appearance and see them as potential (usually hetero)sexual partners, regardless of whether they themselves or the students are married or with partners. Indeed, the practice of married lecturers having serial sexual encounters with female students is so embedded in the cultural mores of academic life that it could almost be positioned as a 'privilege' of the occupation (see for instance Malcolm Bradbury's *The History Man*).

During selection and assessment procedures (for staff as well as students it seems) there are numerous accounts of men making remarks about an applicant's body. As Kagan and Lewis's (1990a) reports of conversations in a psychology department in the UK demonstrate:

(At interview)

FEMALE STAFF:   Are you ready to interview another prospective student yet?

MALE COLLEAGUE:   Yes. What have you got there? I don't want just anyone – give me another of those pretty little girls.

FEMALE STAFF:   Have you got the rest of the application forms there?

MALE COLLEAGUE:   You don't need to see them. All we need to know is if they've got long blonde hair and big boobs.

(At assessment)

FEMALE STAFF:   I'm not sure which student hasn't handed in her essays yet.
MALE COLLEAGUE:   You must know. Brown hair. So ugly you wouldn't even want to mug her.

Male American university staff appear to have similar expectations about the *raison d'être* of female students, which comes as a shock to the young women involved. Carter and Jeffs (1995: 17) refer to one American study which revealed that 26 per cent of male academics admitted to sexual involvement with female students.

In another study, one woman recounted the following:

My whole feeling about surviving in a large university was to get to know my faculty members, so that when they were grading the papers, they were dealing with a person. So I'd always try to meet the people who were teaching my courses. When I went about doing that, one of my professors made an appointment for me to come to his office in the evening. I didn't think anything was weird about it. It wasn't convenient, but everybody had busy schedules. But when I got down there, it was quite clear that he has something else in mind. And it was very hard to figure out how to react. He kissed me, and I didn't know what to do at first. I got slightly involved, and then I thought, wait a minute: this is really weird. And I found a way to get out of the office and back to my dormitory. Clearly if I'd been willing, we'd have had sex right there on the floor of his office.

(Carroll, 1994: 65)

A woman, ambitious and serious about her university education and future career, was seen by the lecturer in the framework of *his* needs as offering herself sexually. He was incapable, it seemed, of treating a woman as anything other than as a sex object – not as a peer, or potential peer.

Lesbian women are often doubly at risk. Although they themselves may never feel tempted to begin a relationship with a man at work, their sexuality is no protection against men's advances. Lesbians are further in jeopardy of harassment and ridicule from both their male and female colleagues if their sexuality becomes publicly known (Kitzinger, 1994). However, their experience of prejudice and censure may depend on the level of hierarchy they have risen to. Single marital status (even if they are not actually without a long-term partner) had for some lesbian women been perceived by their superiors as indicators of flexibility as they were free of the trammels of heterosexual lifestyles. One woman in a study of lesbians in management felt that because she was perceived as more masculine she was sometimes given more stimulating and challenging tasks (Hall, 1989).

## Consensual sex

To find wanted sexual attention, you have to give and receive a certain amount of unwanted sexual attention. Clearly, the truth is that if no one was ever allowed to risk offering unsolicited sexual attention, we would all be solitary creatures.

(Roiphe, 1993)

Roiphe's aim in writing the above quote was to challenge what she saw as the feminist prescription of asexuality implicit in campaigns against date-rape and sexual harassment. Her analysis, however, is limited by what must be her lack of experience of gender relations on campus. While there is little doubt that certain anti-sexual-harassment procedures, such as detailed checking by men as to whether they are causing offence to women in everyday conversation, are insulting to most people, by emphasising the extremes of political correctness there is a danger in trivialising the power of male sexuality. However, to make the simplistic point that many men see women as sex objects may obscure the complexity of sexuality and gendered relationships. Just because women are seen by some men and patriarchal culture in this way, does not mean that men do not fall in love or that women themselves do not have sexual desire. Nor does it mean that some women are not prepared to take advantage of these processes, or find the idea of sex with a powerful man, *per se*, exciting.

It would not be uncommon for a heterosexual female student to express the view that her lecturers are more exciting and interesting intellectually than the young men who are fellow students. She may also feel that she is singled out and special because of her relationship with the lecturer. The dilemma is that this type of sexual liaison is often not based on mutual understanding of why each party is involved.

When you're in a relationship where there's a significant disparity of power, the weaker person is drawn by the attention. In a university situation, of course, the excitement that comes from an intellectual relationship combines with the excitement of a potential sexual relationship. For me it was enormously confusing, and I didn't know what to do with it.

(Carroll, 1994: 65)

The confusion occurs because the relationship takes place within a structure that in itself is more constraining to the parties involved than are the mores of patriarchy. In everyday life, when people meet outside the workplace, it is likely that a woman will have a relationship with a man who is in a senior position to her own, that he will wield more power at work than she will and that he will earn more (Church and Summerfield, 1995). Men reach the top quicker than women in all spheres of professional life.

However, if the individuals concerned are in the same organisation, each participant will know of the other's power-position in relation to themselves. This applies whether or not they are in the same department. Working together makes a sexual relationship even more intriguing, risky, exciting and potentially dangerous. The man, by virtue of being in a senior position, will also *know* more than the woman does about how the organisation works, structurally, formally and in terms of the informal interpersonal level, at least for those involved at the top of the hierarchy. He may also have more experience and/or specialised knowledge of their profession. He will move in social and professional circles with others who are senior to her. She therefore has much to gain informally from such a sexual liaison.

It is frequently suggested that women who have sexual relationships with male bosses have an advantage over other women and their male peers (MacKinnon, 1979). Some men see women as gaining an unfair advantage. In my own medical student research for instance, in answer to the question about whether female students had advantages over men, we often gained the response that middle-aged consultants were likely to give pretty young women priority in selection to junior house officer jobs, and in some cases better marks (Nicolson and Welsh, 1992). However, if this is the case, their advantage is relatively short lived:

> Despite the indications that few benefits redound to the woman who accedes, much folklore exists about the woman who 'slept her way to the top' or the academic professional woman who 'got her degree on her back'. These aphorisms suggest that women who are not qualified for their jobs or promotions acquire them instead by sexual means . . . . Since so few women get to the top at all, it cannot be very common.

(MacKinnon, 1979: 37–38)

In fact women who do engage in sexual relationships at work with senior men rarely achieve in this way (Hearn and Parkin, 1987). When the relationship ends, it is the woman who loses her power or her job (Gutek, 1989).

If a woman is having a relationship with a senior man (or lecturer in the case of a student), she is unlikely to experience a sense of privilege in her everyday life. Indeed, she is likely to have to negotiate greater obstacles than she would if she were not in the relationship. Celia Morris (1994) clarifies this point from her interviews with professional women.

> The trap many women fall into is the belief that giving themselves sexually makes them safer. Behind the romantic folderol attached to sex lies the conviction that it is finally what a man wants and needs from a woman, and that when she has allowed herself to be most vulnerable, he will protect her. In this way, sex becomes the most precious thing a woman has and her ultimate weapon in a precarious world.
>
> (Morris, 1994: 85)

However, as Morris goes on to demonstrate, this happens only rarely. Usually at the end of a relationship a woman is 'unceremoniously dumped' (Morris, 1994: 85).

Some women believe the myth themselves. One woman, an American working as a lecturer in a prestigious medical school, who was seen and saw herself on the 'fast track', actually started an affair with a man she suspected would get the post of Chair in her department.

> I knew he'd get the chairmanship. So whether my motivation for developing an affair with him was based on just my sexual friskiness or on the fact that I thought I'd have an advantage in a very cut-throat system, I can't really tell. I'm ambitious enough that if I'd thought that sex would get me anywhere, I'd probably have done it.
>
> (Cutrer, 1994: 91)

However, when she wanted the affair to end, he did not, and she was forced to have sex with him in order to gain promotion. According to Cutrer, 'We had sex and I got the raise' (p. 91).

She continued to have sex with him when he demanded it, and this lasted for nearly three years. Then she was able to reorganise her working life so she did not need to have contact with him. Only then could the relationship stop.

Sexual or sexualised romance in organisations stimulates emotion, not only in the two participants, but in the potential audience. Colleagues who are aware of an affair at work may believe it distorts communication, trust and power relationships. As Carter and Jeffs (1995) propose, sexual relationships in university departments pollute the social context by creating tensions of various kinds.

> As one mature [female] student put it: 'I could not believe what was going on. I gave up a good job to come here for training. I was shocked to find lecturers regularly using their power to seduce students'.
>
> (Carter and Jeffs, 1995: 16)

The complications of illicit relationships in a university context are numerous. Do colleagues who find out 'blow the whistle'? Carter and Jeffs interviewed someone who saw their head of department out with a student miles away from the university town. Although that person had not said anything, s/he contemplated resignation because of the feeling that the head of department had since become difficult to work with and, it seemed, waiting to catch his witness out.

Lecturer–student liaisons also rouse an element of envy from other students through expectations that the woman will be given privileges over them because of her relationship. Other members of staff, who may have wanted a relationship with the same student, or who themselves do not behave in that way but secretly would like to do so, may also feel envious or resentful. Fellow students of both sexes are made to feel uncomfortable in seminars when the tutor and his girlfriend are present.

## Boys will be boys

It seems that despite both women and men being sexual beings, it is only men who are able to reap the benefits from sex at work. Women who achieve at work frequently are seen as having 'used' their sexuality, while men are seen as being 'natural' or as having been 'used' by the woman (Gutek, 1989).

Lynne Segal (1994) argues that recognition of women's equality in every sphere of life can only occur as a consequence of the demolition of '[hetero]"sexuality" as confirmation of "manhood"' .... Its discursive displacement is central to the battle against the hierarchical gender relations which it serves to symbolise' (Segal, 1994: 317).

The pervasive notion that male equals activity/potency, and female equals passivity/responsiveness lends weight to the 'normality' of sexual exploitation at work, where boys will be boys and for whom sex is part of their legitimate pursuit.

Purkiss (1994), in re-examining the concept of the 'lecherous professor', draws attention to the university as a site for male academic sexual exploitation of female students. It is not only the ethical interpersonal issues that are at stake.

Frequently the man's worth and ability are set directly against the wrongs afflicted on the woman who complains of sexual exploitation. Majorie Carroll, mentioned above, found this out the hard way when she went to complain about the behaviour of her lecturer who had tried to have sexual intercourse with her:

> four of us went to see the head resident, who was a graduate student living in the dormitory, and explained . . . he told us not to say anything because this faculty member was up for tenure and we could get him into trouble! This was an area in which I'd intended to major, and I ended up shifting my field of study because I knew I couldn't deal with this and didn't want to have to. So as a result, I changed what I was concentrating on as an undergraduate. And he got tenure.
>
> (Carroll, 1994: 65)

Two accounts in the UK *Times Higher Education Supplement* raised similar issues:

> One Equal Opportunities officer who spoke to a vice-chancellor about a professor who had been involved with a string of students was informed he was a leader in his field, an asset the university could not afford to lose. It was then made abundantly clear that she was employed to calm the students and not upset the professor in the process.
>
> (Carter and Jeffs, 1995: 16–17)

> I was extremely reluctant to bring a complaint against the tutor. I did so only because I could not face any more tutorials with him, and yet I had to if I were to pass that paper. . . . I did complain. And here I was very lucky. [A female tutor] took it seriously.
>
> (Sanders, 1995: 16–17)

### Blue stocking, virgin or executive tart?

> Searching for a desire of their own – free from entanglement with male-centred myths and meanings – led some heterosexual feminists to abandon longings for physical and emotional intimacy with men.
>
> (Segal, 1994: 214)

Experiencing feminism and heterosexuality as contradictory, many women have opted for a separation between their public life – as strong feminists, as women who work with other women – and their personal life. A feminist might

be very attached to a man who is not without his faults . . . . Once I practically
had to force a woman I worked with for years to introduce me to the man whom
I knew was her partner.

(Valverde, 1985: 62)

Women traditionally, were not only assumed to be asexual socially, but also
biologically and psychologically, in that they neither desired nor experienced
pleasurable sensations through sexual behaviours. Sex and the pursuit of sex,
was for the man's pleasure and for reproduction.

(Nicolson, 1994a: 8)

What are the costs to a professional woman in avoiding being the object of
male desire? Is it possible for a woman to be seen as having a choice about
how to conduct her sexuality? The paradoxes surrounding female
sexuality and its representation have been well documented frequently
by feminist writers (Ussher, 1989; Jeffreys, 1990). Women as a group are
seen under patriarchy as either the virgin/Madonna figure or the loose
woman/whore. These images, however, have had to be 'updated' to apply
to professional women who do not fit easily into either category. Because
they work in the intellectual, active world of men they cannot be the
virginal/Madonna figure perched on her pedestal, and are unlikely to be
taken seriously for long if they are seen as the whore. There is a problem in
expressing any sexuality at all, as may be seen from the preceding sections
of this chapter. As Ehrenreich and English (1979) explained, traditionally
the more competent a women was intellectually, the less likely she was to
be seen as fecund. This potential for sterility was considered to be socially
dangerous.

Thus, in the late twentieth century, as women begin to achieve in their
professions or rise up the management hierarchy, they make themselves
sexually 'invisible'. Women who are in senior positions consciously try not
to be identified as or mistaken for a secretary, the universally sexual being,
where the 'boss–secretary relation should be seen as an important nodal
point for the organisation of sexuality and pleasure' (Pringle, 1989: 162).

Thus women need to desexualise themselves while not being seen as
'men'. This occurs through careful attention to dress on the one hand,
and, equally important, in relation to verbal and non-verbal communication. Women in this position have to avoid both flirting and gestures
that imply subordination, but neither must they appear aggressive.

Sheppard (1989) summarises some of the 'advice' literature thus.
Women's clothing has to avoid drawing attention to her body, but must
not look too much like the male business suit either. She must not be seen
leaving a business meeting to use the toilet, nor should she be seen
purchasing a sanitary towel from the women's toilets as this reminds

witnesses that she may have menstrually related moods; she should be careful that the language she uses is not about bodies; and she should be aware of the kinds of pictures she uses in her office. 'A painting of a cavalry charge or a steam locomotive would probably be too masculine: a watercolour of a meadow with a lot of pastels might be too feminine. Hang only neuter art' (Sheppard, 1989: 150).

However, if a powerful woman, despite careful attention to all these details, transgresses a major patriarchal rule and compromises a man in some way, she is 'put down' via her sexuality. The example of the journalist Ginny Dougary makes this point.

As Dougary recounts in her book *The Executive Tart and other Myths* (1994), she interviewed Norman Lamont (the former British Chancellor of the Exchequer) for *The Times*. Lamont was indiscreet about the Prime Minister, which Dougary duly reported. She was astonished to read the accounts of herself as the journalist, which seemed to overtake media and public concern about the comments of the former Chancellor about the Prime Minister. She was described as

> a 'flame haired', 'alluring' temptress who had enticed poor, helpless Norman into a 'tender trap' using those shameless, age-old feminine wiles. Dougary had even, or so I read [of herself] 'won Norman's heart'. Ah, of course, that must be why she got a good interview.
>
> (Dougary, 1994: 242)

She describes how, as the weeks passed, the Lamont affair became know as 'Lunchgate', and that David Mellor (an ex-Tory Minister, sacked for sexual transgressions) made a vitriolic attack on her (and other women journalists) in a piece in *The Guardian* called 'Who needs old harridans?', where he compares Lynn Barber, whom he refers to as 'a sabre-toothed old harridan who by the look of her has lived a bit, and none too wisely either', to Ginny Dougary: 'the sorceress's apprentice . . . . Quite what it is in Ms Dougary's CV that qualifies her for all this advanced super-ciliousness is beyond me. But I'm steering clear of her, and I suspect after this, even old Norman will too' (Dougary, 1994: 242–243). With this quote Dougary ends her book – need one say more?

## SEXUAL HARASSMENT

> Sexual harassment, most broadly defined, refers to the unwanted imposition of sexual requirements in the context of a relationship of unequal power.
>
> (MacKinnon, 1979: 1)

Sexual harassment is the 'unsolicited non-reciprocal male behaviour that asserts a woman's sex role over her function as a worker.'

(Benokraitis and Feagin, 1995: 31)

Sexual harassment is any unsolicited and unwelcome sexual advance, request for sexual favours, comment or physical contact when such a contact has the purpose or effect of unreasonably interfering with an individual's work or academic performance or of creating an intimidatory, hostile or offensive working or academic environment.

(Nicolson and Welsh, 1992[1])

Sexual harassment, verbal, physical and visual, poisons the atmosphere of any organisation. Sexist calendars, jokes, personal remarks about women's bodies, groping and rape all occur in organisations and have been well documented (Brant and Too, 1994).

All organisations, throughout their hierarchies, containing men from all social class groups, are hosts to acts of sexual harassment, and despite its recent identification as being 'against the rules', complaints procedures are invariably problematic (see, for example, MacKinnon, 1979; Chapter 5 and in this chapter above).

The first legislation against sexual harassment at work appeared in the United States in the second half of the 1970s (European Parliament, Working Paper, 1994) and many of the early cases have been outlined by MacKinnon (1979). The European Community is taking legislation about sexual harassment seriously and aims to ensure that all member countries have adequate legislation and complaints procedures (European Parliament Working Paper, 1994).

There is, however, no doubt that the behaviour and motivation of the perpetrators are complex and the experiences of the victims are traumatic and long-lasting, not least because of the ramifications of making a complaint and the enduring harassment or the need to change jobs if the victim does not complain.

Even those women who have the motivation and stamina to bring a complaint to court have to endure similar ordeals to victims of rape, although in sexual harassment cases their identities, details of their sexual histories and current lifestyle are made public, which is humiliating. This is compounded if the victim loses her case – as with Anita Hill vs. Judge Clarence Thomas in the United States. (However, despite her experience of losing, having her reputation challenged and the threat of public humiliation, Anita Hill inspired and provided comfort to a great many women both in the USA and the rest of the world; Morris, 1994.)

Sexual harassment is a serious offence. It is akin to threat and intimidation as the hundreds of case studies which have been recorded now testify (see MacKinnon, 1979; Wise and Stanley, 1987; Morris, 1994; Brant and Too, 1994). Not all feminist writers agree, however. Roiphe (1993) states that:

> Our female professors and high-ranking executives, our congress-women and editors, are every bit as strong as their male counterparts. They have earned their position of authority. To declare that their authority is vulnerable to a dirty joke from someone of inferior status just because that person happens to be a man is to undermine their position. Female authority is not (and should not be seen as) so fragile that it shatters at the first sign of male sexuality. Any rules saying otherwise strip women, in the public eye, of their hard-earned authority.
>
> (Roiphe, 1993: 90)

But as I set out in this book, life is more complex. The constant exposure to sexism is an over-riding reason why more women are not in authority, and those that do reach senior positions often sacrifice their feminine identity and relations with other women to do so. Men ensure that junior men are protected from the threat of a challenge from women and feminism in general. But if we take Roiphe seriously, then women who achieve seniority will continue to take the role of Queen Bee with no regard for the health and welfare of those who follow or her female peers.

## SEXUAL ABUSE, GENDER AT WORK AND THE CARING PROFESSIONS

If sexual harassment is treated as a 'normal' part of working life, and greater concern is offered to the accused whose career might suffer than to the victim, there is little chance that sexual abuse at work is taken seriously.

The female body remains a generalised object of sexual pleasure for men (Snitow et al., 1984; Ussher, 1989), and the persistent portrayal of erotic images has its influence on, and is influenced by, symbolic meanings, which are culturally pervasive (Martin, 1989). (See Chapter 3.)

It is sometimes difficult to distinguish between sexual abuse and sexual harassment. Both are about exploitation of (usually) women by (usually) men in a context where the man has power over the woman's work or life. Examples of sexual harassment at work ranged from pictures of naked women on office walls to multiple rape (see Anderson et al., 1993). So is there a difference?

One example was provided by a group of women doctors at a seminar on sexual harassment I ran for Women in Medicine. One woman told me that when she had been a junior doctor attached to a gynaecological team, one male gynaecologist was known to fondle and abuse the bodies of women undergoing surgery. He would remark on their shape, the tautness or otherwise of their vaginas, and play with their breasts. He would also leave them uncovered when this was not necessary. On one occasion, he used the patient's vagina gratuitously as a 'container' for a surgical instrument. He then made a joke, and the doctor telling me the story was so angry that she had told him his behaviour was totally unacceptable. He ignored her comments, but ten minutes later made a general remark to the team that most of them needed a consultant's reference for their next job if they seriously wanted a career. I was the only person at the seminar who was shocked by this story. The other women doctors present were able to confirm that they had witnessed similar behaviour on several occasions by male surgeons in relation to anaesthetised female bodies.

But what motivated this man and other abusers like him? The intent on the part of the perpetrator seems to be to gain and maintain sexual and political power over (and possibly have sex with) the victim. Neither abuse nor harassment can be about mutual affection, although in cases of both, some perpetrators have declared their love (see Morris, 1994).

One distinction that has been used is that *harassment* happens to women who are in a context where the men concerned may be in senior roles, but they only have power over the working life of that woman. *Abuse* occurs to girls/women when the perpetrator has a major influence over the victim's life and her physical and/or emotional well-being (Raitt, 1994). Thus a parent, or parent-figure such as a school teacher, can be a sexual abuser.

However, the health professional, psychotherapist or social worker who exploits their access to power over adult women's bodies and minds, also perpetrates abuse. Sue Llewellyn (1992), in her review of the literature on the sexual abuse of clients by therapists, found that the majority of abuse was from men to women, with around 10 per cent of male therapists admitting to having sex with patients and up to 80 per cent of these repeating their behaviour. Intimacies between physicians and patients occur regularly despite professional ruling against such behaviours and the risk of being debarred from practice (Kardener, 1974; Gartrell et al., 1986).

Health and social work professions are among those with high numbers of women aspiring to and achieving senior positions. The fact of sexual abuse raises dilemmas for professional women in these perverse patriarchal organisations.

## Whistle blowing

Rosemary, a clinical psychologist, had been friendly with Jeremy, her colleague for several years. In fact he had been instrumental in helping her get appointed to the clinic, and supported and encouraged her through two promotions. She was also friendly with his wife.

She inadvertently discovered him one evening in an embarrassing and clearly sexual embrace with a female client, and was posed with the dilemma of how to handle her discovery. He was clearly abusing his client by taking advantage of his privileged knowledge of her vulnerabilities, the power of his role in relation to her, and also presumably deceiving colleagues and his wife. Rosemary, as a health professional, was deeply concerned for the welfare of the patients in the care of psychologists in general and her clinic in particular, as well as being shocked by the inappropriate and unprofessional conduct of her friend.

After much discussion and soul searching she told Jeremy that she had no option other than to report his behaviour. He became very angry with her, trying to tell her that the relationship with the patient was really one between equals and was thus none of Rosemary's business. However, she did tell their boss, who reprimanded Jeremy, who promised that he would not behave that way again. In the meantime though, Rosemary received an angry telephone call from Jeremy's wife (who she had not wanted to hear of these events). Jeremy's wife accused Rosemary of jealousy and of being a busybody. When she repeated her story at a discussion about sexual abuse in therapy, she was wondering whether she had been right to report Jeremy, but no-one at the conference left her in any doubt that she had been right. Rosemary, however, still believes that she suffered more from the censure of being labelled as 'disloyal' to a colleague than Jeremy did from being reprimanded for abuse.

## The toxic context

The problems faced by professional women (such as hospital doctors, lawyers, academics) in dealing with sexual harassment, abuse and discrimination are, first, the behaviours that constitute sexual harassment may be masked or appear less serious than those experienced by women in lower status occupations. Professional organisations (e.g. hospitals, universities, legal practices, professional associations, schools) tend to have norms of behaviour which prohibit overt and violent actions that would be reported to the police, fire service and so on.

On the whole, for professional women, sexual harassment is likely to be verbal and low key. Thus the victim's plight is likely to be invisible, and the overall ethos of 'not rocking the boat' will be applied against anyone who complains about harassing behaviour that on the surface is not impinging on the work environment. Thus, as with Anita Hill, there is a public demonstration of ambivalence towards the female victim (Morris, 1994). Frances Conley, a neurosurgeon at Stanford University medical school, who resigned in protest against a persistent sexual harasser being appointed to head her department, is quoted as saying:

> What women put up with in the medical field is more subtle. But it can be just as devastating because it happens far more frequently, it's pervasive, and it's a cultural thing. It's like a ton of feathers. We all get hit daily by a feather of verbal abuse dropping on us.
>
> (Conley, 1994: 111)

Second, and clearly related to the first, is that women correctly believe their careers will suffer if they complain, and thus despite being privileged over the part-time, semi-skilled workers in material ways, they have potentially more to lose and so keep quiet or at least take anonymous action. An account in the *British Medical Journal* in October 1992 (*BMJ* 1992) in which a female doctor recalled a series of events (meeting with an older colleague who grabbed her bottom; another one who would brush against junior women, enter colleagues' rooms at night and offer to swap duties for sex; having her complaints that some lecturers' slides or comments were sexist and gratuitous, dismissed) which to her made it clear that the medical establishment was saturated with sexism and sexual harassment, but that there was little support to enable anyone to complain overtly.

Third, women in the professions, by virtue of their numbers and the organisational/professional ethos are unlikely to get support from a peer group.

It is, therefore, important to acknowledge both that personal assertiveness and organisational mechanisms for dealing with sexual harassment are not adequate for combating the problem; indeed, they may result in a culture that dismisses its existence – 'because if it happened we would know about it wouldn't we?'

## CONCLUSIONS

Sexuality is part of everyday life and professional organisations are far from being 'safe havens'. It may be argued that work organisations are among the most sexually explicit social contexts (Hearn and Parkin,

1987). It is, however, difficult to disentangle sexuality from gender–power relations, and although there is no attempt to assume universal heterosexuality by that observation, there is little doubt that heterosexual men set the sexual and power agendas in professional life.

## NOTE

1   The operational definition used in our survey adapted from the University of Sheffield guidelines.

# Part III

# Challenging patriarchy
## No Man's Land?

# Introduction to Part III

Senior women in management and the professions are caught in a dilemma: they are isolated from other women both because they are few in number and because most women do not achieve or aspire to achieve high levels of professional success. However, they have to fight harder than men to maintain and improve on their success and, as I have argued above, there is limited support for women under patriarchy.

Most women who are in senior roles reject feminist ideology, theory and practice. However, analysis of their positions within patriarchal organisations may only be accomplished within a feminist framework. Non-feminist perspectives make gender, and thus the experience of women *as women*, invisible.

In the final section of this book I attempt to draw together feminism, subjectivity, biography and psychoanalysis to make sense of women's lives in a professional context. In doing this, the aim is to develop a model, not only for survival, but for individual and organisational growth in connection with gender equality.

In Chapter 7, 'Barriers, boundaries and emotion', I examine the psychological consequences of the complex gender differences in emotional connectedness between women and men. What strategies do each employ for survival? How do women in senior roles cope with their marginalisation and isolation in organisational life?

The chapter begins by reiterating the contrasting patterns of psychological development between women and men as careers develop and individuals confer a meaning on their lives through accounting for themselves biographically. It contrasts the coherence between male success and masculine identity with the divergence between feminine success and feminine identity. Women remain marginal to the grand narrative of career success and organisational power. While this is the result of patriarchal power relations, it ensures that women distance themselves from feminism and other women.

Chapter 8, the concluding chapter, examines ways of putting feminist psychology into practice. It is argued that the only way that individual women, and organisations themselves, will benefit is for friendship and co-operation between women to continue to develop as these enable connectedness and reflexivity.

# Chapter 7

# Barriers, boundaries and emotion
## Gender, power and meaning

## INTRODUCTION

There are undeniably visible differences between women and men's expectations, attitudes and behaviour in relation to work organisations, and these distinctions solidify as individuals rise up the hierarchy. Men either push for career success and achieve seniority or they come to terms with having underachieved or deviated from social expectations. Women's experience is more complex. Socialisation into femininity is not as clear cut as masculinity and women do not have expectations of certain success (see Chapter 4). Thus women who find the going too tough may resign from the organisation, or at least drop out of the fast track, do so with fewer regrets than might men (see Marshall, 1994). Women who do succeed in management or the professions are more likely to *increase* the problems and stress in their lives than if they opt out (Davidson and Cooper, 1983), and the more senior a woman becomes she is more likely to be stressed at work than a man of equivalent seniority (Cushway, 1991). There are good social reasons why women find the high flying life difficult, particularly if they are mothers (see e.g. Cooper and Lewis, 1993). However, there are additional difficulties for senior women, particularly in relation to the management of *psychological boundaries* between self, social context and their sense of gendered subjectivity (see Chapter 2). To be doing 'male' things in patriarchal organisations and wanting to achieve in this arena does not preclude the desire to be feminine or to enjoy being a woman and being seen as a woman with a sexual, intellectual and emotional presence that is feminine.

It is important to reiterate that while not subscribing to an essentialist perspective on gender differences and gendered behaviours, it is clear that women and men give different meanings to their bodies and experience differential socialisation in such a way that it becomes difficult to disentangle what women do because they are born female, and what they do because of complicated cultural processes (see Chapters 3 and 4).

In this chapter I explore how women and men negotiate boundaries between self, other, organisation and culture. Women in a patriarchal context need to be able to distinguish between their sense of subjectivity/ self, cultural and interpersonal expectations and the meaning given to their organisational contribution by others *because they are women*. It is difficult to have control over the latter but it is vital to recognise through the process of reflexivity that those meanings exist, and also that boundaries are dynamic and shift from occasion to occasion.

## DYNAMICS OF THE DEFERENTIAL DIALECTIC

The first psychological demand that flows from a woman's social role is that she must *defer* to others, follow their lead, articulate her needs only in relation to theirs. In essence, she is not to be the main actor in her own life. As a result of this social requirement, women come to believe they are not important in themselves for themselves. Women come to feel they are unworthy, undeserving and unentitled. Women are frequently self-deprecating and hesitant about their own initiatives. They feel reluctant to speak for themselves, to voice their own thoughts and ideas, to act on their own behalf. Being pushed to defer to others means that they come to undervalue and feel insecure about themselves, their wants and their opinions. A recognition of a woman's own needs can therefore be complicated and a process occurs in which women come to hide their desires from themselves.

(Eichenbaum and Orbach, 1982: 29)

The women described in preceding chapters initially would not seem to fit into the social role requirements outlined above. However, closer inspection (and indeed introspection) indicates that much of what Eichenbaum and Orbach say resounds with reality. They are but providing a psychological baseline onto which women's career socialisation, reflexivity and biography have become inscribed.

There is no persuasive evidence of essential, immutable female characteristics which make deference a prerequisite for women's biographical development. However, as Bell and Newby (1976) noted twenty years ago, sexual stratification is about 'the relationships between the sexes rather than the attributes of one sex or the other' (p. 152). While Bell and Newby focused their attention on husbands and wives, a similar perspective is crucial for understanding the relationships between the sexes in organisations, where people frequently spend years co-existing, competing, supporting and forming relationships with others who just happen to work together rather than choosing to share their lives. Bell and

Newby identify the 'relational and normative means by which men (particularly husbands) maintain their traditional authority over women (wives), and...the necessary strategies they employ in attempting to ensure the *stability* of their power' (Bell and Newby, 1976: 152, original emphasis). They argue that many wives believe their husbands have – and ought to have – more power than they do, and legitimatisation of this in traditional values leads to the hierarchical nature of the relationship between husband and wife as seeming natural and immutable. This position is echoed in studies of women and men in management and the professions, particularly some of the boss–secretary, student–lecturer relationships described in Part II.

The existence of a tradition whereby men hold professional power serves to legitimatise it, and for many women this implies and becomes manifest in their deference to a senior manager/professional who is also a man. Individual women who achieve power in their own right have challenged this, but their challenge does not deprive men of apparent legitimate authority in the eyes of other men and women. Many women, even senior and aspiring women, still exhibit non-assured, deferential qualities.

Indeed, it is alarming to observe how far professional women's accounts of their subjectivity in organisational life concurs with this image. Tanton (1994), discussing a workshop series on developing women's presence in senior management, said:

> Some other reasons were given as to why we need to develop women's presence. These referred to particular characteristics which women needed or lacked, for example, assertiveness, aggression, self-esteem, confidence, and so on. For example they said 'women are less aggressive', 'women lack self-esteem'. The focus of the group was on woman as 'other' to the characteristics of the male norm. This could be interpreted as pragmatic given that they worked in what they described as 'male-dominated' organisational cultures.
>
> Alternatively it could be seen as a measure of the depth of the entrenched values within society that even this group of women concentrating their attention on the issue of women's development approached it from the perspective of the 'centred male'.
>
> (Tanton, 1994: 9)

So even senior and aspiring women recognise, in certain contexts at least, that they are outside the central arena for organisational action, either by virtue of deliberate exclusion or because they 'lack' the necessary qualities. This reinforces the potential, at least, for women's deference.

But why is this still the case even for women who appear to have overcome the socialisation process of the patriarchal organisational culture and achieve success?

Women display deference because of ongoing patterns of subordination of women/girls to men/boys, which is part of a relationship pattern based on power dynamics in the family, socialisation and cultural belief systems that are inescapable without taking on the mantle of outcast. It is not difficult to see or reflect upon the way that being seen and treated as subordinate and gaining recognition through deference may set up a template for social relations, both in the family and in professional organisations. If women feel insecure about their talents and abilities because of their socialisation and gender–power relations inherent in the dominant culture, they will develop a range of coping/survival strategies to deal with this insecurity (see Marshall, 1984; Cassell and Walsh, 1991). This involves them attempting to negotiate their subjectivity and interpersonal relationships as though they were *other* than women. However, despite the claims of many women interviewed in studies of managers and businesswomen, this position has social, and consequently psychological, difficulties. This is in part because:

> The second requirement of woman's social role is that she must always be *connected* to others and shape her life according to a man. A woman's status will derive from that of her mate. Indeed her very sense of self and well-being may rely on their connection.
>
>                    (Eichenbaum and Orbach, 1982: 29, original emphasis)

A woman not connected with a man, presenting herself as independent, is treated with suspicion, whether that independence is at home or at work. In Chapter 6 there was evidence that some women are connected to men who are their seniors in sexualised ways, whether emotionally, through sexual harassment, exploitation or even when they believe themselves to be exploiting their heterosexuality in an organisational context. The sexualised nature of the work relationship carries over from this heterosexual connectedness where women identify with their immediate bosses or senior men. However, this connectedness is often the means of acting out a deferential relationship because the man is the superordinate one.

## SELF, SUBJECTIVITY AND OTHERS

Eichenbaum and Orbach (1982) suggest that deference and connectedness to others naturally leads on to 'another psychological concomitant of women's social role: that of having emotional antennae. A woman must learn to anticipate others' needs' (p. 29). Subjectivity for women appears to contain far greater complexity than subjectivity for men, and for women in senior management and in the professions this complexity is exaggerated by the apparent stepping outside of the boundaries of feminine behaviour.

In chapters 3 and 4 it was argued that, socially and psychically, men are separated from their mothers and identify not specifically with individual fathers but with all men (Freud, 1922; Chodorow, 1978). Masculine identity is treated more seriously, and greater efforts are made by agents of socialisation to ensure that boys do not step outside the boundaries of 'natural' masculine behaviour (Archer, 1989). On the other hand, women remain connected to their mothers and fathers in different ways, and feel guilt and anxiety about asserting their own needs. This process relates to women's professional roles too (see chapters 3 and 4).

Much has been written about the differences in masculine and feminine leadership style. Frequent assertions are made about the benefits women as managers provide for their colleagues and junior staff, especially because of their ability to focus on and deal with emotional issues (see, for instance, O'Leary and Ryan, 1994, for a summary). This still does not mean that women are *valued* for their feminine qualities, nor is there much effort to understand the pressures of both having emotional antennae and coping with patriarchal organisations (Tanton, 1994).

## Boundaries and connectedness

A secure sense of boundary between 'self' and 'other' in effect means that an individual is able to enter relationships, connect appropriately with the other person/people, engage with the organisation and remain subjectively secure, while having contributed to and benefited from the social and emotional exchange. Almost everyone experiences a degree of ego vulnerability at certain times, although some do so far more than others. People who feel empty unless they are in love, those (such as John discussed in Chapter 4, who project all their unacceptable feelings outwards) are examples of those who have fragile egos and a fluid sense of boundaries between themselves and others as well as the good and bad feelings in themselves. Poor boundary definition means that the individual is in constant danger of becoming overwhelmed both by their own feelings and actions and those of others. For many, particularly women, reflexive about their organisational role, there is evidence of struggles to identify the boundaries between home and work, self and organisation, self and gender role, being a senior corporate executive and a feminist, and so on. Boundary issues are important for everyone, and the process of reflexivity discussed in Chapter 2 along with notions of durée, biography and different levels of consciousness all point to the centrality of *conscious self-awareness* in the process of psychological survival. I shall return to and expand on this point below.

Object relations theory in psychoanalysis, which refers to the work of Klein, Fairbairn, Guntripp and Winnicott, was particularly useful in identifying the importance of psychological–emotional boundaries in ego development. Simply stated, the infant, initially connected with her/his mother, fails to perceive separation (see Chapter 4 for details of Klein's perspective). This develops gradually with the strength and maturity of the ego. The adult understands itself to be separate as an individual, but this does not always translate itself into an emotional awareness. The social nature of subjectivity (see Chapter 2) additionally suggests that the 'person' is also connected socially and culturally to others (see, for example, the work of Wendy Hollway and Valerie Walkerdine in *Changing the Subject, 1984*).

However, there seems to be an important gender difference in the management of boundaries at work. There is an interesting tension between boundary management and 'barrier' management, with senior men and some women more skilled at the latter than discursively aware of the former.

In my discussions with various male friends and colleagues in senior management positions, two characteristics emerged. First was the deliberate effort (usually successful) to ignore the needs of individuals in order to achieve management goals, and, second, was the fascination with 'feminine' insights, which were often asked for to provide 'commentary' on their constructions of the organisation.

I conjecture that the former represents their ability to construct barriers between self and others (although reasonably effective managers are able to see over them!) which help them to survive the interpersonal rigours of organisational life, and the latter, in a more complex way, ensures that women enable men to manage their own boundaries. This interaction is frequently practised by men to uphold their own ego strength when the barriers waver, and by women to gain access to power and information through attachment and connectedness.

There are many examples of this. A manager in a university department, excellent at identifying talent and able to support women he believed had the appropriate qualities for promotion, was surprised when his secretary resigned, accusing him of insensitivity. Other junior academic staff, particularly women on short-term research contracts, also saw him as a 'brute'. He, however, had enough insight into his own management style to tell me that if he worried about such things then he would go under himself. He had become immune, although he failed to see why the woman in question did not see the world as he did. His priority was to make the unit effective, while keeping staff motivated. He was selective about choosing who to mentor, and they tended to be those who shared similar points of view with him. However, this did not stop his curiosity about interpersonal life in the department, although this was merely 'interesting' rather than essential to his management role. When the junior staff left, he saw them as exploiting a career opportunity elsewhere, and never considered whether the possibility that he might have handled them better had any relevance.

Another man, who had recently been appointed in a senior position in an insurance company with the specific purpose of increasing 'efficiency', told me with some pride that he was completely unable to recognise emotional responses in his staff and believed that was his strength. He did, however, complain to me that various people made a habit of 'whinging'. For example, he had engineered a staff redeployment exercise involving a move to another site, which was a long way from where many of the junior administrative and secretarial staff had worked before and was the other side of town from where they lived. He claimed to be inundated with trivial complaints about car parking facilities and the late arrival of the internal mail. He told me in some detail how he had personally been to see those responsible for the mail circulation and found very little difference between the timing of deliveries in the previous building and the new one. 'Why do I have to listen to this garbage?' he asked. I suggested it might have more to do with how they *felt* they had, and continued to be, treated than the timing of the mail and the car parking. He was intrigued, claiming that such ideas had never occurred to him, and we had a discussion about this, which he appeared to find interesting. However, it did not change his behaviour, nor even his evaluation of the issues involved.

On reflection, I think that we were both engaging in a complex interaction of power, deference and connectedness, which at the time was of mutual benefit, but provided little in the way of long-term change in either of our opinions or, if we had been working in the same institution, power relations. I was flattered that such a senior and influential person appeared to value my opinion, which also gave me a sense of connectedness to him and to power. He found my insights interesting and my attention emotionally supportive. But while I thought that I was having an influence on the decisions he might make, or how he might handle some of his staff, he was simply intrigued. He was achieving confirmation of his power, and not taking my information and advice at face value.

This behaviour is also typical of managers and professionals working in the same organisation. The senior man survives through defending himself from emotional onslaughts by denying their significance in the organisational goals. When there are occasions that some of these feelings might be overwhelming, he seeks to talk to a woman he trusts. This enables the woman to employ connectedness and emotional/nurturing skills and gain access and insights into senior management, possibly not available to her in the formal hierarchical structure. The man, however, continues to develop high status strategic ideas with his male friends and colleagues and sees the emotional contact as secondary to the real purpose of management.

This means that the woman gains some of her ambitions – access to information and aspects of power – but the relationship rarely contributes to her career in terms of mentoring or role modelling because the man is taking 'time out' from the real concerns, while she believes she is sharing them.

It is not only psychoanalysis that helps understand or identify these processes. Conversation analysis and the interpretation of gestures provides clues on interaction and meaning. Deborah Tannen, in her work on gender and language, draws attention to disparities in meanings which women and men assume are shared. She considers that a man is likely to engage in the world

> as an individual in a hierarchical social order in which he was either one-up or one-down. In this world conversations are negotiations in which people try to achieve and maintain the upper hand if they can, and protect themselves from others' attempts to put them down and push them around.
>
> (Tannen, 1993: 24–25)

She argues that men's lives are about maintaining independence and avoiding failure. Thus they are able to exploit necessary resources, including their female friends and colleagues, and believe others to be doing the same.

A woman, on the other hand, Tannen argues, approaches the world 'as an individual in a network of connections. In this world conversations are negotiations for closeness in which people try to seek and give confirmation and support, and to reach consensus' (Tannen, 1993: 25). This does not mean that women do not have other goals, such as protecting themselves, but while men protect themselves from challenge, women protect themselves from others' attempts to exclude them and avoid isolation.

There are no essentialist gender differences involved here – this is part of differential socialisation and expectations (see chapters 3 and 4). There are rewards for both the men and women involved in these exchanges which are based on friendship, mutual respect and, probably, sexuality in many cases.

If psychoanalysts, from Freud, Chodorow and Horney to Orbach and Eichenbaum, are correct, then women experience a greater fluidity in their sense of subjectivity and their boundaries with other people than do men. To be emotionally aware and *need* connection with others, for many women, is part of being human. They see the world in terms of social relationships, and it is only because of the widespread acceptance that male-dominated, patriarchal knowledge has the 'real' value that some women deny such understandings. So phenomena such as 'instinct' and 'female intuition' are ridiculed or downplayed and seen as unsound, unscientific knowledge, when in fact there is much anecdotal evidence to suggest that intuition pays off in the management of people and understanding organisational life as frequently as any more 'objective' understanding of human interactions.

## EMOTION

Maintaining ego strength is not simply a routine and intellectual project. To make sense of your self in a paradoxical context (that is, one you wish to belong to but one in which you are also marginal) is fraught with emotional pitfalls. Loneliness and isolation are emotionally laden experiences, and the desire for and achievement of independence and autonomy cannot compensate for lack of intimacy, support and connectedness. It is the latter that enables self-reflection and maintenance.

It is only relatively recently that attention has been paid to the role of emotion in organisations (Fineman, 1993), although psychoanalytically inclined management projects have at least identified unconscious forces such as guilt and anxiety at work (see DeBoard, 1978).

It is no surprise to learn that women are seen as emotional and men as rational, and that rationality is valued over emotionality (see Swan, 1994). As a consequence, emotion is kept out of sight in the organisational world, and although some members are expected to exhibit emotion, they are the marginal, dispensable or inadequate staff. 'Emotion is to be expected in the less powerful such as interviewees and appraisees but the competent manager must herself remain unemotional' (Swan, 1994: 90).

It is, however, clear that the category 'emotion' is a flexible one, and under certain circumstances emotion is seen as acceptable and even laudable. This is when it is associated with men, especially senior men. Thus the professor who choked back the tears on his retirement celebration was seen as 'human', and his distress and sadness at leaving his colleagues made up for past power struggles and previous contentions.

There are sometimes different emotions expressed by women and men as a response to the same event. On receiving the news that they had been passed over for promotion, Ian and Angela, two well considered academics, met to express their outrage. Ian was furious and told his friend and colleague how he was undervalued, that he knew himself to be far more competent than colleagues who had already been promoted and that he would immediately look for another post, at which time he would make his current university bid against their competitor to keep him. He was not prepared to experience such a rejection again. Angela, equally furious, said how she was also extremely upset and felt that this rejection also made her feel undervalued. She kept thinking of how much more she needed to publish before next year's round of promotions, and wondered whether she was really up to that task. If her own university would not promote her, would she stand a chance of being appointed elsewhere? When they had finished their discussion she became even more gloomy and downhearted, while Ian maintained his anger.

In this example, not only does the woman temper her anger with personal hurt and upset, but the failure to promote her is taken as an evaluation of her self-worth rather than an exercise in distributing limited rewards in a highly competitive situation. The hurt of rejection seeps through her ego boundary and influences her self-evaluation. This in turn leads her to be depressed and despondent. Ian, on the other hand, did not appear emotionally influenced by the board's decision. He also expressed genuine amazement that Angela, whom he admired, had made that interpretation.

Men also do express emotion in organisations about professional matters, but in hidden ways. In engaging in sexual relationships, for example, men, particularly senior men, have the opportunity to expose and consider their vulnerabilities in a safe context (or at least one that is safe for the duration of the affair). Younger men are sometimes able to turn to older women in ways that they could not turn to other men, and even if the woman is their senior they are able to engage in an invisible emotional relationship.

As an example, a senior male colleague of mine, with whom I was working on a project, once told me that meeting with me was like taking confession with a Catholic priest. He found himself telling me things about his feelings and his understanding of his relationships with others in the university, almost against his will. He sometimes became angry and upset, and other times excited or amused with the things he was relating. My motivation in this relationship was that I liked him and would ask about the kinds of things that I would normally discuss with my women friends. It seems that these were clearly not on the agenda in conversations he had with other people. The need for his emotions to be invisible outside the 'confessional' made him a difficult person to work with, from my perspective. He would sometimes be impossible to contact, my messages with important queries about our work were only half answered, and every so often his secretary would phone to arrange an appointment which would be unnecessary if he had responded to my written messages. He preferred to come to my office rather than meet in his own, and the pattern of our meetings would be some business and much emotional discussion. I clearly colluded with this pattern, but partly because, as in previous examples, my role gave me some influence, information and access to power. It was the secrecy of my role that perplexed me. There was no question of a sexual advance. However, it began to make sense once I began the thinking and the reading for this book.

### Hidden conflict and women's work

Sometimes women's informal role in the emotional life of an organisation is called upon more directly. Deborah Kolb wrote:

> I often find myself drawn into conflicts at work. Colleagues come in, close the door, and then confide in me about some problem they have with a mutual associate or boss. I listen and, probably more often than is wise, agree to take the matter up with the other person(s). Sometimes I succeed in altering the situation and at other times I report back what I have learned. I often wonder why I get involved. Is it because I am accessible – my door is usually open – or because I relish good gossip or because people know of my interest in mediation or because they think I will make a difference? Whatever the reasons for my own involvement, I have recently become aware of how pervasive this kind of informal peacemaking is.
>
> (Kolb, 1992: 63)

As a result she conducted research on informal peacekeeping in organisations, a task which seems to fall on senior- or middle-ranking women. Kolb argues that whereas formal conflict resolution is well researched and a well respected, vital role in an organisation (although it may be the case that outside consultants are brought in to achieve these ends), informal peacemaking, particularly the kind she talks about, is almost forced to be invisible and as such appears to hold no merit and has no value in the organisational culture. Yet for those who take that role, or have it put upon them, it is consuming of time and energy, although as Kolb herself accepts, it does have certain rewards. However, in her research she is forced to conclude that the women respondents 'seem to contribute to a gendered construction of their activities as unimportant and, ironically, to the reproduction of a gender-based system of relation-ships in organisations' (Kolb, 1992: 68).

Her respondents acted as go-betweens between senior managers and other senior or up-and-coming staff (sometimes between men). They shared several characteristics: they were located in positions in the organisation that enabled them to learn about emerging conflicts and problems. They provided a sympathetic ear. They felt non-threatening, easy to talk to and sensitive to interpersonal conflicts. They believed that gender was important and that women were seen, and were able, to take this peacekeeping role. Also, the women in Kolb's study were in specific positions which gave them access to power. One was married to a senior manager, another shared an interest with the company president but was herself not in the management hierarchy, and the third was an academic, one of the very few senior, tenured women at the university and known for taking women's issues seriously. All believed in their abilities and enjoyed their role.

## ISOLATION

> *Intimacy* is a key in a world of connection where individuals negotiate complex networks of friendship, minimise differences, try to reach consensus, and avoid the appearance of superiority, which would highlight differences. In a world of status, *independence* is key, because a primary means of establishing status is to tell others what to do, and taking orders is a marker of low status. Though all humans need both intimacy and independence, women tend to focus on the first and men on the second.
>
> (Tannen, 1993: 26, original emphasis)

Even though it is unlikely that *all* women's and men's behaviour and needs may be always demarcated in such a way, there is increasing support for the view that psychological and social factors conspire to achieve these gender differences. The specific difficulty that this imposes upon the lives of senior professional women is that while they are likely to have developed skills which resemble those of male executives (see earlier chapters in this book as well as, for example, Marshall, 1984; White et al., 1992; McKenzie Davey, 1993), there is something missing. There is no-one with whom they are able to share intimacy. There are few opportunities for making the number or the same quality of pragmatic relationships in corporate life as men who relate to other men. While they are likely to have achieved an ability for independence there is nothing to moderate it, and instead of being independent, they are lonely and isolated.

Sheppard (1992) found that female managers perceived themselves to be isolated in a variety of contexts, and much of this related to the way that organisational culture reflects male styles and interactional needs (see Chapter 5). 'Women can't take for granted with whom they can associate, as they perceive political consequences that may devolve from even the most casual or informal contacts' (Sheppard, 1992: 156). They have to be careful of relationships with men that may be misconstrued as sexual (see Chapter 6) or of friendships that might be misconstrued as supportive instead of career-oriented (see above in this chapter).

The female managers in Sheppard's research sample also stressed that they felt a lack of support from male colleagues and that there was a need for a network of women managers. This again suggests a recognition of the mismatch in gender-related needs. More important in their sense of isolation was that, by definition, the women managers needed to detach themselves from being identified with women in clerical and secretarial posts and those in junior roles in the organisation. Thus, as Tanton (1994) concludes, the life of a female senior professional or manager is exceptionally cruel because she is both deprived and has to deprive herself of most opportunities for intimacy and connectedness.

Tanton continues by suggesting that the experience of isolation and loneliness may lead on to further uncomfortable issues operationalised by role descriptions. She summarises some from earlier studies:

- boundary-marker. . . 'where she treads the men may not wish to go' – 'she represents the outside';
- *extra-visible manager*. . . 'if she puts a foot wrong she will be noticed';
- *traitor*. . . 'other women criticise my differentness [through promotion] from them';
- *martyr*. . . 'I have to go on and on or I'll let my women colleagues down';
- *one of the boys* 'I don't have any problems – I feel just like a man';

- *conformist* 'conformity and the abandonment of critical consciousness are the prices of successful performance in the bureaucratic
  world' . . . ;
- *unrecognised explorer* 'I have to go where no other women have been
  but there's little recognition when I get there'.

(Tanton, 1994: 19–20)

It is having to take on the mantle of outsider, stranger, or marginal person
in one of these guises that contributes to the stress levels of women
managers and professionals (Davidson and Cooper, 1983; Marshall,
1994).

To cope with isolation and loneliness, barriers have to be erected. Men
have opportunities of support from women to overcome the potential for
desolation and emotional bleakness that strong barriers and the maintenance of power precipitate. Women do not have the same opportunities
because they cannot afford to obtain support from junior women. This is
partly because they need to be seen as different from the junior women
and partly because junior women's expectations of them are likely to
weigh them down as much as support them (see Chapter 4).

To cope with being a woman in a man's world, women have to manage
boundaries between themselves and other women, between themselves
and men, and between themselves and the organisation culture – that is
patriarchy. Are they selling out? Are they losing their femininity? Are they
exploiting their sexuality? Are they doing their job well? These issues have
to be managed constantly if the woman professional is to survive in a form
that she herself recognises and respects. She has constantly to redefine her
own boundaries. Promotion and success mean personal growth, and that
is the benefit of rewarded talent and ambition. However, for women, out
of place in patriarchal organisations, it is imperative that they reassess
their relationship with themselves – to reflect on the 'me' (self as object, as
described in Chapter 2) and to find a means of maintaining and enhancing
ego-strength.

## CONCLUSIONS

In order to achieve in their professions and negotiate successfully the
intrigues of corporate life, men and women have adopted differential
strategies for psychological survival. Men find grafting the attributes of
early sex-role socialisation to be more straightforward in this enterprise
than do women. Femininity, intellectual ability and competitiveness do
not fit easily with beliefs about career success. In addition, women *are*

women – they have learned to be feminine, to negotiate the world in a feminine way and have no reason not to value that. However, the predominant norms of organisational culture conflict with, or at least severely undervalue, the norms and expectations associated with being a woman. Women have to redefine themselves, both to negotiate organisational culture while maintaining their sense of femininity and as far as possible being true to their own subjective beliefs.

Women are frequently in close relationships with their male colleagues, but there is both anecdotal and research evidence to suggest that there are frequent misunderstandings of the function of these relationships because of gender–power expectations and beliefs.

# Chapter 8

# Conclusions

## INTRODUCTION

[Women and men live different lives and have different careers. It frequently takes many years of trial and error before an individual woman is able to recognise this and identify the implications for her own working experience. As men hold the authority in all professional organisations, the burden falls on women to make sense of the culture and its constraints and develop suitable coping strategies. The result is that women commonly find individualised means of survival (Marshall, 1984; Cassell and Walsh, 1993; McKenzie Davey, 1993), which gives rise to both the myth and the reality of the Queen Bee or 'Female Barracuda' (Ussher, 1990b; Morris, 1994). A self-fulfilling prophecy may be involved; to survive a woman has both to fail other women and isolate her emotional self from men.

Power is, by nature, a rare commodity and beyond the grasp of most women and men, but still it is almost exclusively in the hands of men. As Celia Morris (1994) proposes therefore, 'It should come as no surprise . . . that women have looked on other women as rivals in the competition for scarce resources – whether for men, positions or esteem – or that they've scapegoated those who try to do things differently' (p. 233).] But, as argued in the earlier chapters, there is little future in being an isolated woman, however outstanding that makes an individual feel. There are less opportunities for connection or being supported and mentored. The only hope for denting patriarchy is for women to support other women unequivocally.

## WOMEN AND POWER

[ If women are to take their rightful power, there will have to be a vast surge in organisational activities among us. The opposition says derisively that women can't work together; we react to this with terrific defensiveness but we know there is a grain of truth in the charge. Something unique to women often leads women-to-women organisations into failure.

(Wolf, 1994: 307)

Women need other women, and thus have to support each other. There is no point in saying 'there are no women in my organisation' – that is the thin end of the wedge. Women in senior positions need other women alongside them, and to achieve this they need to do something about recruiting, training and promoting other women.

While corporate and political efforts have gone into persuading organisations of the need to do the latter, there is not much evidence that women have changed their views to others. Senior women rarely call themselves feminists (Kitch, 1994) and thus take the male view of behaviour and knowledge for granted, which, as I argued in Chapter 1, pathologises women.

It is the male view that women cannot work together. Wolf (1994) is right, women do believe that to be the case, and that is the predominant myth. But many men cannot work together either. Some senior and influential men refuse contact with an enemy or rival, others play dangerous games with the sole intention of damaging their adversary and no concern for corporate welfare. It is women's oppression, isolation and lack of experience that enables the continuation of the belief that women cannot co-operate. If there were more women to choose from as allies, and if women did not take the quality of relationships as seriously as they do, then this myth would be assuaged.

## WOMEN'S SUPPORT AND RESISTANCE

Feminists have grown up with the idea of various kinds of support group, but for those for whom feminism is anathema, it is likely that such groups might seem equally repugnant. The first action necessary for the isolated female senior professional or executive is to recognise that she is not just a doctor, academic, manager or a lawyer, but, whether she accepts it or not, she is a *woman* doctor, academic, manager, lawyer. Margaret Thatcher, notorious as a British Prime Minister who rejected feminist and women's concerns, to her chagrin has always been described by her gender as well as her rank. As time passes with no female successors, her identification as a woman in that office will be even stronger.

The second action for the senior woman, then, is to ensure that she is succeeded by other women. Men behave in that way, as I have argued.

Men, however supportive of equal rights, still see their prior commitment to carrying on the patriarchal tradition, and thus, consciously or not, mentor, support and promote other men. They see the future as taking root in those who reflect their own image – and so must women. It is hard when there is no tradition, and there is no doubt a need to fight. But instead of fighting alone for promotion, having to work harder and shine brighter than male rivals, surely it makes ecological sense to put energy into supporting other women who in turn will offer reciprocal sustenance?

In the mid-1980s in the UK, a group of women psychologists, mainly in junior academic or postgraduate posts, decided to challenge the British Psychological Society's establishment and set up what later became The Psychology of Women Section (POWS; for details see Burns, 1990). Through working co-operatively, having a common purpose and sharing the tasks and commiseration for defeats on the way to success, the group not only benefited emotionally, but learned a great deal about patriarchal organisations. That was beneficial in itself. However, working together and achieving their explicit aims also gave each member of the group self-confidence and the impetus to carry on working as feminist psychologists.

It was not a perfect group. After the initial setting up of the section, there were various 'falling outs'. However, none now remains in a junior post, a fact that has raised some criticisms from other feminist psychologists, suspecting that the whole endeavour might have been a 'career move'. However, the POWS continues to thrive under a totally new group of women, and whether this new group knows it or not, the opportunities they have now for influencing British psychology were the result of women's achievement through challenging male power, rather than, more typically, male concession to equal opportunities.

Women with career ambitions and others who have achieved seniority share a history, a biology, a culture and a struggle. What has been both surprising and obvious in my experience of working alongside, as well as supervising, other women from similar and different professional backgrounds is that whatever the starting point, the game turns out to be the same. It is about gender, power and patriarchy. It operates under different disguises, but women are always outside the main arena, however far they have attempted to be part of the culture. That can only change if we recognise that men fear our strength, not our isolated presence.

# References

Aitkenhead, M. and Liff, S. (1990) 'The effectiveness of equal opportunities policies', in J. Firth-Cozens and M.A. West (eds) *Women at Work*, Milton Keynes: Open University Press.

Alimo-Metcalfe, B. (1992) 'Gender and Appraisal: Findings from a National Survey of Managers in the British National Health Service', paper presented at the Global Research Conference on Women in Management, Ottawa.

—— (1994) 'Waiting for fish to grow feet! Removing organisational barriers to women's entry into leadership positions', in M. Tanton (ed.) *Women in Management*, London: Routledge.

Anderson, R., Brown, J. and Campbell, E.A. (1993) *Aspects of Sex Discrimination in Police Forces in England and Wales*, London: Home Office.

*BMJ* (1992) 'Personal view: unprofessional behaviour', *British Medical Journal*, 305, 962.

Apter, T. (1993) *Professional Progress: Why Women Still Don't Have Wives*, Basingstoke: MacMillan.

Archer, J. (1986) 'Gender roles and developmental pathways', *British Journal of Social Psychology*, 23, 245–256.

—— (1989) 'Childhood gender roles: structure and development', *The Psychologist*, 9, 367–370.

—— and Lloyd, B. (1982) *Sex and Gender*, London: Penguin.

—— and Rhodes, V. (1993) 'The grief process and job loss: a cross-sectional study', *British Journal of Psychology*, 84, 395–410.

AUT (1990) *Goodwill Under Stress: Morale in UK Universities*, London: Association of University Teachers.

Aziz, A. (1990) 'Women in UK Universities: the road to casualisation?', in S. Stiver Lie and V.E. O'Leary (eds) *Storming the Tower: Women in the Academic World*, London: Kogan Page.

Beckett, H. (1986) 'Cognitive developmental theory in the study of adolescent development', in S. Wilkinson (ed.) *Feminist Social Psychology: Developing Theory and Practice*, Milton Keynes: Open University Press.

Bee, H. (1981) *The Developing Child*, 3rd edn, New York: Harper and Row.

Bell, C. and Newby, H. (1976) 'Husbands and wives: the dynamics of the deferential dialectic', in D. Barker and H. Allen (eds) *Dependence and Exploitation of Women in Work and Marriage*, London: Longman.

Beloff, H. (1992) Study reported in the *Times Higher Education Supplement*, 17 April, 5.

Bem, S.L.(1974) 'The measurement of psychological androgyny', *Journal of Consulting and Clinical Psychology*, 42, 155–162.

—— (1981) 'Gender schema theory: a cognitive account of sex typing', *Psychological Review*, 88, 354–364.

—— (1993) *The Lenses of Gender*, London: Yale University Press.

Benokraitis, N.V. and Feagin, J.R. (1995) *Modern Sexism: Blatant, Subtle and Covert Discrimination*, 2nd edn, New Jersey: Prentice Hall.

Berger, P. (1966) 'Identity as a problem of knowledge', *Archives europeaennes de sociologie*, 7, 105–115.

—— and Kellner, H. (1964) 'Marriage and the construction of reality', in M. Anderson (ed.) *Sociology of the Family*, Harmondsworth: Penguin, 1982.

—— and Luckman, (1985) *The Social Construction of Reality*, Harmondsworth: Pelican.

Bernard, J. (1981) *The Female World*. New York: The Free Press.

Bettelheim, B. (1979) *The Informed Heart: Autonomy in a Mass Age*, New York: Avon.

Bhavnani, K. and Phoenix, A. (1994) *Shifting Identities Shifting Racisms*, London: Sage.

Bion, W. (1961) *Experiences in Groups*, London: Tavistock.

Birke, L. (1986) *Women, Feminism and Biology: The Feminist Challenge*, Hemel Hempstead: Harvester.

Bleier, R. (1984) *Science and Gender: A Critique of Biology and Its Theories on Women*, Oxford: Pergamon.

Bocock, R. (1983) *Sigmund Freud*, London: Tavistock.

Bouchier, D. (1983) *The Feminist Challenge*, Basingstoke: Macmillan.

Bradbury, M. (1979) *The History Man*, London: Arrow Books.

Brant, C. and Too, Y.L. (1994) *Rethinking Sexual Harassment*, London: Pluto.

Breakwell, G.B. (1985) *The Quiet Rebel: Women at Work in a Man's World*, London: Century.

Brennan, T. (1992) *The Interpretation of the Flesh*, London: Routledge.

—— (1993) (ed.) *Between Feminism and Psychoanalysis*, London: Routledge.

BMA (1993) *Patronage in the Medical Profession*, London: British Medical Association.

British Psychological Society (1990) 'Sexual Harassment and Unethical Intimacy between Teachers and Trainees: Discussion and Policy', unpublished document, The Division of Criminological and Legal Psychology Training Committee.

Brittan, A. (1989) *Masculinity and Power*, Oxford: Blackwell.

Broverman, I.K., Broverman, D.M., Clarkson, F.E., Rosenkrantz, P.S. and Vogel, S.R. (1970) 'Sex role stereotypes and clinical judgments of mental health', *Journal of Consulting and Clinical Psychology*, 34, 1–7.

Burman, E. (1989) 'Feminisms and Feminists in Psychology', paper presented at the Critical Psychology Symposium, British Psychological Society's London Conference.

—— (1990a) *Feminists in Psychological Practice*, London: Sage.

—— (1990b) 'Differing with deconstruction', in I. Parker and J. Shotter (eds) *Deconstructing Social Psychology*, London: Routledge.

—— and Parker. I. (1993) *Discourse Analytic Research: Repertoires and Readings of Texts in Action*, London: Routledge.

Burns, J. (1990) 'Women organising within psychology', in E. Burman, (ed.) *Feminists in Psychological Practice*, London: Sage.

—— (1992) 'The psychology of lesbian health care', in P. Nicolson and J.M. Ussher (eds) *The Psychology of Women's Health and Health Care*, London, Macmillan.

Burton, C. (1991) *The Promise and The Price*, Sydney: Allen and Unwin.

Buss, D.M. (1994) 'The strategies of human mating', *American Scientist*, 82, 238–249.

Butler, A. and Landells, M. (1995) 'Taking offence: research as resistance to sexual harassment in academia', in L. Morley and V. Walsh (eds) *Feminist Academics: Creative Agents for Change*, London: Taylor and Francis.

Campbell, K. (1992) *Critical Feminism: Argument in the Disciplines*, Milton Keynes: Open University Press.

Caplan, P. (1994) *Lifting a Ton of Feathers: A Woman's Guide to Surviving in the Academic World*, Toronto: University of Toronto Press.

Carroll, M. (1994) in C. Morris *Bearing Witness: Sexual Harassment and Beyond. Everywoman's Story*, New York: Little, Brown and Company.

Carter, P. and Jeffs, T. (1995) 'The Don Juans', *Times Higher Education Supplement*, 10 March, 16–17.

Cassell, C. and Walsh, S. (1991) 'Towards a Woman-friendly Psychology of Work: Gender, Power and Organisational Culture', paper presented to the British Psychological Society's Annual Occupational Psychology Conference, Liverpool University.

—— (1993) 'Being seen but not heard: barriers to women's equality in the workplace', *The Psychologist: Bulletin of the British Psychological Society*, 6 (3), 110–114.

*Changing the Subject* (1984) London: Methuen (collective).

Chetwynd, J. and Hartnett, O. (1978) *The Sex Role System*. London: Routledge and Kegan Paul.

Chodorow, N. (1978) *The Reproduction of Mothering*, Berkeley: University of California Press.

—— and Contratto, S. (1982) 'The fantasy of the perfect mother', in B. Thorne and M. Yalom (eds) *Rethinking the Family: Some Feminist Questions*, New York: Longman.

—— (1994) *Femininities, Masculinities and Sexualities: Freud and Beyond*, London: Free Association Books.

Choi, P.Y.L. (1994) 'Women's raging hormones', in P.Y.L. Choi and P. Nicolson (eds) *Female Sexuality: Psychology, Biology and Social Context*, Hemel Hempstead: Harvester.

—— and Nicolson, P. (1994) (eds) *Female Sexuality: Psychology, Biology and Social Context*, Hemel Hempstead: Harvester.

Church, J. and Summerfield, C. (1995) *Social Focus on Women*, London: HMSO.

Cockburn, C. (1993) *In the Way of Women: Men's Resistance to Sex Equality in Organisations*, Basingstoke: Macmillan.

Collinson, D. and Hearn, J. (1994) 'Naming men as men: implications for work, organisation and management', *Gender, Work and Organisation*, 1 (1), 2–22.

Condor, S. (1991) 'Sexism in psychological research: a brief note', *Feminism and Psychology*, 1 (3), 430–434.

Conley, F. (1994) in C. Morris *Bearing Witness: Sexual Harassment and Beyond. Everywoman's Story*, New York: Little, Brown and Company.

Connell, R.W. (1993) *Gender and Power*, Cambridge: Polity Press.

Cooper, C. and Lewis, S. (1993) *The Workplace Revolution: Managing Today's Dual Career Families*, London: Kogan Page.

Coote, A. and Campbell, B. (1982) *Sweet Freedom*, London: Picador.

Coward, R. (1993) *Our Treacherous Hearts*, London: Faber and Faber.

Coyle, A. (in press) 'Using the counselling interview to collect research data on sensitive topics', *Journal of Health Psychology.*

Crawford, D. (1989) 'The future of clinical psychology: whither or wither?', *Clinical Psychology Forum*, 20, 29–31.

Crawford, M. and Maracek, J. (1989) 'Psychology reconstructs the female: 1968–1988', *Psychology of Women Quarterly*, 13, 147–166.

Cushway, D. (1991) 'Stress in Clinical Psychologists', paper presented at the British Psychological Society's Annual Conference, Bournemouth.

Cutrer, P (1984) in C. Morris *Bearing Witness: Sexual Harassment and Beyond. Everywoman's Story*, New York: Little, Brown and Company.

Davidson, M.J. and Cooper, C.L. (1983) *Stress and the Woman Manager*, Oxford: Martin Robertson.

—— and (1992) *Shattering the Glass Ceiling: The Woman Manager*, London: Paul Chapman.

—— and (1993) (eds) *European Women in Business and Management*, London: Paul Chapman.

Davidson, N. (1988). *The Failure of Feminism*, Buffalo, New York: Prometheus Books.

DeBoard, R. (1978) *The Psychoanalysis of Organisations*, London: Tavistock.

DeLameter, J. and Fidell, L.S (1971) 'On the status of women', in L.S. Fidell and J. DeLameter (eds) *Women in the Professions: What's All the Fuss About?*, London: Sage.

Delmar, R. (1986) 'What is feminism?', in J. Mitchell and A. Oakley (eds) *What is Feminism?*, Oxford: Blackwell.

Department of Health (1991–2) 'Medical and dental staffing prospects in the NHS in England and Wales 1990', *Health Trends*, 23, 4, 132–141.

Doherty, K. (1994) 'Subjectivity, Reflexivity and the Analysis of Discourse', paper presented at the British Psychological Society London Conference, University of London Institute of Education.

Dougary, G. (1994) *The Executive Tart and Other Myths*, London: Virago.

Dryden, C. (in press) *What About Marriage? Psychology, Gender Relations and Feminism*, Hemel Hempstead: Harvester.

Dworkin, A. (1992) *Pornography*, London: The Women's Press.

Eagley, A.H. (1987) *Sex Differences in Social Behaviour: A Social Role Interpretation*, Hillsdale: Erlbaum.

Ehrenreich, B. and English, D. (1979) *For Her Own Good: 150 Years of the Experts' Advice to Women*, London: Pluto.

—— (1983) *The Hearts of Men*, New York: Pluto.

Eichenbaum, L. and Orbach, S. (1982) *Outside in . . . Inside Out*, Harmondsworth: Penguin.

Eisenberg, C. (1989) 'Medicine is no longer a man's profession', *New England Journal of Medicine*, 321, 1542–1544, quoted in G. Silver (1990) *The Lancet*, 335, 1149–1150.

Elston, M. (1993) 'Women doctors in a changing profession: the case of Britain', in E. Riska and K. Wegar (eds) *Gender, Work and Medicine*, London: Sage.

Erikson, E. (1968) *Identity, Youth and Crisis*, London: Faber and Faber.

European Parliament Working Paper (1994) *Measures to Combat Sexual Harassment in the Workplace*, Luxembourg: Directorate General for Research.

Evetts, J. (1994) (ed.) *Women and Career: Themes and Issues in Advanced Industrial Societies*, London: Longman.

Faith, K. (1994) 'Resistance: lessons from Foucault and feminism', in H.L. Radtke and H.J. Stam (eds) *Power/Gender*, London, Sage.

Faludi, S. (1992) *Backlash*, London: Vintage.

Fidell, L.S. and DeLameter, J. (eds) (1971) *Women in the Professions: What's All the Fuss About?*, London: Sage.

Fierman (1990) 'Do women manage differently?', *Fortune*, 122 (15), 115–118.

Fineman, S. (1993) (ed.) *Emotion in Organisations*, London: Sage.

Firth-Cozens, J. and West, M.A. (1990) (eds) *Women and Work*, Milton Keynes: Open University Press.

—— (1991) 'Sources of stress in junior house officers', *British Medical Journal*, 301, 89–91.

Flanders, M.L. (1994) *Breakthrough: The Career Woman's Guide to Shattering the Glass Ceiling*, London: Paul Chapman.

Fogarty, M.P., Allen, I. and Walters (1981) *Women in Top Jobs*, London: Heinemann Educational Books.

Forster, P. (1992) 'Sexual Harassment at work', *British Medical Journal*, 305, 944–946.

Foucault, M. (1973) *The Archaeology of Knowledge*, London: Tavistock.

—— (1978) *The History of Sexuality*, Vol. 1, Harmondsworth: Penguin.

—— (1980) *Power/Knowledge: Selected Interviews and Other Writings 1972–1977*, Brighton: Harvester Press.

Fox, N.J. (1993) *Post Modernism, Sociology and Health*, Milton Keynes: Open University Press.

French, J.R.P. Jnr and Raven, B.H. (1959) 'The bases of social power', in D. Cartwright (ed.) *Studies in Social Power*, Ann Arbour: Univeristy of Michigan.

Freud, S. (1921) 'Group psychology and the analysis of the ego' in Vol. XVIII of *The Standard Edition of the Complete Psychological Works of Sigmund Freud*, 65–143, London: Hogarth.

—— (1922) 'Some neurotic mechanisms in jealousy, paranoia and homosexuality', in Vol. XVIII of *The Standard Edition of the Complete Psychological Works of Sigmund Freud*, 22–232, quoted in T. Brennan (1992) *The Interpretation of the Flesh*, London: Routledge.

—— (1925) 'Some psychical consequences of the anatomical distinction between the sexes', in *On Sexuality*, Harmondsworth: Penguin, 1977.

—— (1931a) 'Female sexuality', in *Three Essays on the Theory of Sexuality* (trans. J. Strachey), New York: Norton, 1977.

—— (1931b) 'Female sexuality', in The Pelican Freud Library, Vol. 7, *On Sexuality*, Harmondsworth: Penguin, quoted in R. Bocock (1983) *Sigmund Freud*, London: Tavistock.

—— (1933) *New Introductory Lectures in Psychoanalysis* (trans. J. Strachey), New York: Norton, 1965.

—— (1973) 'Femininity', Lecture 33 in *New Introductory Lectures on Psychoanalysis*, Vol. 2, Harmondsworth: Pelican.

Frosh, S. (1992) 'Masculine ideology and psychological therapy', in J.M. Ussher and P. Nicolson (eds) *Gender Issues in Clinical Psychology*, London: Routledge.

—— (1994) *Sexual Difference: Masculinity and Ideology*, London: Routledge.

Fursland, E. (1993) 'Veterans of the consulting room share their traumas', *The Independent*, 8 June.

Gannon, L. (1994) 'Sexuality and the menopause', in P.Y.L. Choi and P. Nicolson (eds) *Female Sexuality: Psychology, Biology and Social Context*, Hemel Hempstead: Harvester Wheatsheaf.

Gartrell, N., Herman, J., Silvia, O., Feldstein, M. and Localio, R. (1986) 'Psychiatrist-patient sexual contact: results of a national survey, I: prevalence', *American Journal of Psychiatry*, 143 (9), 1126–1131.

Geertz, C. (1979) 'From the native's point of view: on the nature of anthropological understanding', in P. Rabinow and W.M. Sullivan (eds) *Interpretive Social Science*, Berkeley, University of California Press.

Giddens, A. (1979) *Central Problems in Social Theory*, Basingstoke: Macmillan.

—— (1984) *The Constitution of Society*, Cambridge: Polity Press.

—— (1993) *The Transformation of Intimacy*, Cambridge: Polity.

Gilligan, C. (1982) *In a Different Voice: Psychological Theory and Women's Development*, Cambridge MA: Harvard University Press.

Goldin, C. (1990) *Understanding the Gender Gap: An Economic History of American Women*, Oxford: Oxford University Press.

Griffin, C. (1989) 'I'm not a women's libber but . . . . Feminism, consciousness and identity', in S. Skevington and D. Baker (eds) *The Social Identity of Women*, London: Sage.

—— (1995) 'Feminism, social psychology and qualitative research', *The Psychologist*, 8 (3), 119–121.

Grosz, E. (1990) *Jacques Lacan: A Feminist Introduction*, London: Routledge.

Gutek, B. (1989) 'Sexuality in the workplace: key issues in social research and organisational practice', in J. Hearn, D.L. Sheppard, P. Tancred-Sheriff and G. Burrell (eds) *The Sexuality of Organisation*, London: Sage.

Hall, M. (1989) 'Private experiences in the public domain: lesbians in organisations' in J. Hearn, D.L. Sheppard, P. Tancred-Sheriff and G. Burrell (eds) *The Sexuality of Organisation*, London: Sage.

Halton, W. (1994) 'Some unconscious aspects of organisation life: contributions from psychoanalysis', in A. Obholzer and V.Z. Roberts (eds) *The Unconscious at Work*, London: Routledge.

Hansard Society Commission (1990) *Women at the Top*, London: Hansard Society for Parliamentary Government.

Harding, S. (1986) *The Science Question in Feminism*, Milton Keynes: Open University Press.

Hargreaves, D. (1986) 'Psychological theories of sex-role stereotyping', in D.J. Hargreaves and A.M. Colley (eds) *The Psychology of Sex Roles*, London: Harper and Row.

Harré, R. (1993) Foreword to J. Shotter's *Cultural Politics of Everyday Life*, Milton Keynes: Open University Press.

—— Clarke, D. and DeCarlo, N. (1985) *Motives and Mechanisms: An Introduction to the Psychology of Action*, London: Methuen.

—— and Gillett, G. (1994) *The Discursive Mind*, London: Sage.

—— and Secord, P.F. (1972) *The Explanation of Social Behaviour*. Oxford: Blackwell.

Hearn, J. and Parkin, W. (1987) *'Sex' at 'Work': The Power and Paradox of Organisation Sexuality*, Brighton: Wheatsheaf Books.

Henwood, K. and Pidgeon, N. (1995) 'Remaking the link: qualitative research and feminist standpoint theory', *Feminism and Psychology*, 5 (1), 7–30.

Holland, L. and Spencer, L. (1992) *Without Prejudice? Sex Equality at the Bar and in the Judiciary*, Bournemouth: TMS Management Consultants.

Hollway, W. (1989) *Subjectivity and Method in Psychology*, London: Sage.

—— and Mukarai, L. (1990) 'The Position of Women Managers in the Tanzanian Civil Service', University of Bradford, Report to the Civil Service Department Government of Tanzania.

Horney, K. (1967) *Feminine Psychology*, London: Norton, 1993.

Jaques, E. (1955) 'Social systems as a defence against persecutory and depressive anxiety', in M. Klein, P. Heimann, and R. Money-Kyrle (eds) *New Directions in Psychoanalysis*, London: Tavistock.

Jeffreys, S. (1990) *Anticlimax*, London: The Women's Press.

Kagan, C. and Lewis, S. (1990a) 'Where's your sense of humour? Swimming against the tide in higher education', in E. Burman (ed.) *Feminists in Psychological Practice*, London: Sage.

—— and Lewis, S. (1990b) 'Transforming psychological practice', *Australian Psychologist*, 25, 270–281.

Kaiser, B.L. and Kaiser, I.H. (1974) 'The challenge of the women's movement to American gynaecology', *American Journal of Obstetrics and Gynaecology*, 120 (5), 653 655.

Kardener, S.H. (1974) 'Sex and the physician patient relationship', *American Journal of Psychiatry*, 131 (10), 1135–1137.

Kitch, S.L. (1994) ' "We're all in this alone": Career women's attitudes towards feminism', in C.W. Konek and S.L. Kitch (eds) *Women and Careers: Issues and Challenges*, London: Sage.

Kitzinger, C. (1990) 'Resisting the discipline', in E. Burman (ed.) *Feminists in Psychological Practice*, London: Sage

—— (1992) 'Interview with Sandra Bem: feminist psychologist', *The Psychologist*, 5 (5), 222–224.

—— (1994) 'Anti-lesbian harassment', in C. Brant and Y.L. Too (eds) *Rethinking Sexual Harassment*, London: Pluto.

Klein, M. (1975) *Envy and Gratitude*, London: Hogarth Press, 1993.

Kohlberg, L. (1966) 'A cognitive developmental analysis of children's sex role concepts and attitudes', in E.E. Maccoby (ed.) *The Development of Sex Differences*, California: Stamford University Press.

Kolb, D.M. (1992) 'Women's work: peacemaking in organisations', in D.M. Kolb and J.M. Bartunek (eds) *Hidden Conflict in Organisations*, London: Sage.

Konek, C.W. and Kitch, S.L. (1994) *Women and Careers: Issues and Challenges*, London: Sage.

Lacan, J. (1977) *Ecrits: A Selection*, London: Tavistock.

Laws, S. (1983) 'The sexual politics of pre-menstrual tension', *Women's Studies International Forum*, 6, 19–31.

Lefford F. (1987) 'Women in medicine. Women doctors: a quarter century track record', *The Lancet*, 30 May, 1254–1256.

Lehman, C. (1990) 'The importance of being earnest: gender conflicts in accounting', *Advances in Public Interest Accounting*, 3, 137–158.

Leonard, P. (1984) *Personality and Ideology*, Basingstoke: Macmillan.

Levinson, D. (1986) 'A conception of adult development', *American Psychologist*, 41 (1), 3–13.

Lewis, S.E. (1994) 'The Pathologisation of Gender: The Case of Depression, paper presented at the 2nd International Conference on Qualitative Health Research, Pennsylvania State, USA.

—— (1995) 'The Social Construction of Depression: Experience, Discourse and Subjectivity', unpublished PhD thesis, University of Sheffield.

Llewellyn, S. (1992) 'The Sexual Abuse of Clients by Therapists', paper presented at the British Psychological Society Annual Conference, Scarborough.

Maccoby, E.E. and Jacklin, C.N. (1974) *The Psychology of Sex Differences*, Stanford: Stanford University Press.

McKenzie Davey, K. (1993) 'Women Balancing Power and Care in Early Career: Am I Feminine or Just One of the Lads?', paper presented at British Psychological Society's Psychology of Women Section Annual Conference, University of Sussex.

MacKinnon, C.A. (1979) *Sexual Harassment of Working Women*, London: Yale University Press.

McLoughlin, J. (1992) *Up and Running: Women in Business*, London: Virago.

McNay, L. (1992) *Foucault and Feminism*, Cambridge: Polity.

Maguire, M. (1995) *Men, Women, Passion and Power: Gender Issues in Psychotherapy*, London: Routledge.

Markham, G. (1993) 'When women doctors behave as men' (letter), *British Medical Journal*, 307 (11 September), 686.

Marris, P. (1986) *Loss and Change*, London: Tavistock.

Marshall, H. and Nicolson, P. (1991) 'Why choose psychology? Mature and other students' accounts at graduation', in J. Radford (ed.) *The Choice of Psychology*, Leicester: British Psychological Society.

Marshall, J. (1984) *Women Managers: Travellers in a Male World*, New York: Wiley.

—— (1986) 'Exploring the experience of women managers', in S. Wilkinson (ed.) *Feminist Social Psychology*, Milton Keynes: Open University Press, 193–209.

—— (1994) 'Why women leave senior management jobs', in M. Tanton (ed.) *Women in Management*, London: Routledge.

Martin, E. (1989) *The Woman in the Body*, Milton Keynes: Open University Press.

Maupin, R.J. (1993) 'How can women's lack of upward mobility in accounting organisations be explained?', *Group and Organisational Management*, 18 (2), 132–152.

Mead, G.H. (1934) *Mind, Self and Society*, Chicago: University of Chicago Press.

Medsoc Editorial, Northwing (1991) Sheffield University Students Union.

Mitchell, J. (1974) *Psychoanalysis and Feminism*, Harmondsworth: Pelican.

Molloy, J.T. (1977) *The Woman's Dress for Success Book*, New York: Warner Books.

MORI (1994) 'Sex in the Professions', Report for Hays Personnel Services Ltd.

Morris, C. (1994) *Bearing Witness: Sexual Harassment and Beyond. Everywoman's Story*, New York: Little, Brown and Company.

Morris, P., Holloway, J. and Noble, J. (1990) 'Gender representation within the BPS', *The Psychologist*, 9, 408–411.

Mowrer, O.H. (1950) *Learning Theory and Personality*, New York: Wiley.

NHS Management Executive (1992) *Women in the NHS: An Implementation Guide to Opportunity 2000*, London: NHS Management Executive.

Nicolson, P. (1988) 'The Social Psychology of Post Natal Depression', unpublished PhD thesis, University of London.

—— (1991a) 'Heroines', *Changes: An International Journal of Psychology and Psychotherapy,* 9 (3), 181–182.

—— (1991b) 'Vicki Bruce: Chair of the Scientific Affairs Board', *The Psychologist,* 4 (6), 261–262.

—— (1992a) 'Towards a psychology of women's health and health care', in P. Nicolson and J. Ussher (eds) *The Psychology of Women's Health and Health Care,* Basingstoke: Macmillan.

—— (1992b) 'Menstrual cycle research and the construction of female psychology', in J.T.E. Richardson (ed.) *Cognition and the Menstrual Cycle: Research, Theory and Culture,* London: Springer Verlag.

—— (1992c) 'Feminism and academic psychology', in K. Campbell (ed.) *Critical Feminism: Argument in the Disciplines,* Milton Keynes: Open University Press.

—— (1993a) 'Public values and private beliefs: why do women refer themselves for sex therapy?', in J.M. Ussher and C.D. Baker (eds) *Psychological Perspectives on Sexual Problems,* London: Routledge.

—— (1993b) 'The social construction of motherhood', in D. Richardson and V. Robinson (eds) *Introducing Womens Studies,* Basingstoke: MacMillan.

—— (1993c) 'Doctoring the records', *The Guardian,* 6 September, 11.

—— (1994a) 'Is anatomy destiny? Sexuality and the female body', in P. Choi and P. Nicolson (eds) *Female Sexuality: Psychology, Biology and Social Context,* Hemel Hempstead: Harvester Wheatsheaf.

—— (1994b) 'Deconstructing sexology: the pathologisation of female sexuality', *Journal for Reproductive and Infant Psychology,* 11, 191–201.

—— (1995a) 'The menstrual cycle, science and femininity: assumptions underlying menstrual cycle research', *Social Science and Medicine,* 41 (6), 779–784.

—— (1995b) interview with Nadine Radford, *The Independent* 18 January, 31.

—— (1995c) interview with Geraldine McCool, *The Independent,* 1 March, 30.

—— (1995d) 'Postnatal Depression and the Social Construction of Motherhood', paper presented at the British Psychological Society's Annual Conference, University of Warwick.

—— (1995e) 'Qualitative research and mental health: analysing subjectivity', *Journal of Mental Health,* 4 (4), 337–345.

—— and Welsh, C.L. (1992) 'Gender Inequality in Medical Education', Preliminary Report to Trent Regional Health Authority.

—— and Welsh, C.L. (1993) 'From Larva to Queen Bee', paper presented at the British Psychological Society's Psychology of Women Section Conference, Sussex University.

—— and Welsh, C.L. (1994) 'Undermining Equal Opportunities in Medical Education: The Case of "Blindness" to Sexual Harassment', paper presented at the 8th Conference of the European Health Psychology Conference, University of Alicante.

O'Leary, V.E. and Ryan, M.M. (1994) 'Women bosses: counting the changes or changes that count', in M. Tanton (ed.) *Women in Management: A Developing Presence,* London: Routledge.

OECD (1979) *Equal Opportunities for Women,* Paris: Organisation for Economic Co-operation and Development.

Parker, I. (1993) *Discourse Dynamics: Critical Analysis for Social and Individual Psychology*, London: Routledge.

Parkin, W. (1993) 'The public and the private: gender, sexuality and emotion', in S. Fineman (ed.) *Emotion in Organisations*, London: Sage.

Parlee, M.B. (1990) 'Premenstrual Syndrome and Menstrual Cycle Research', paper presented at a research seminar, University of Sussex.

Philp, M. (1985) 'Madness, truth and critique: Foucault and anti-psychiatry', *PsychCritique*, 1, 155–170.

Pillinger, J. (1993) *Feminising the Market*, Basingstoke, MacMillan.

Potter, J. and Wetherell, M. (1987) *Discourse and Social Psychology*, London: Sage.

Prather, J. (1971) 'Why can't women be more like men?', in L.S. Fidell and J. Delameter (eds) *Women in the Professions: What's All the Fuss About?*, London: Sage.

Pringle, R. (1989) 'Bureaucracy, rationality and sexuality: the case of secretaries', in J. Hearn, D.L. Sheppard, P. Tancred-Sheriff and G. Burrell (eds) *The Sexuality of Organisation*, London: Sage.

Purkiss, D. (1994) 'The lecherous Professor revisited: Plato, pedagogy and the scene of harassment', in C. Brant and Y.L. Too (eds) *Rethinking Sexual Harassment*, London: Pluto.

Radke, H.L. and Stam, H.J. (1994) *Power/Gender*, London: Sage.

Raitt, S. (1994) 'Sexual harassment and sexual abuse: when girls become women', in C. Brant and Y.L. Too (eds) *Rethinking Sexual Harassment*, London: Pluto.

Rapoport, R. and Rapoport, R. (1976) *Dual Career Families Re-examined*, London: Martin Robertson.

Reinhartz, S. (1985) 'Feminist distrust: problems of context and content in sociological work', in D.N. Berg and K.K. Smith (eds) *The Self in Social Inquiry: Researching Methods*. California: Sage.

Reskin B.F. and Padavic I. (1994) *Women and Men at Work*, London: Pine Forge Press.

Richardson, D. and Robinson, V. (1993) Introducing Women's Studies, Basingstoke: MacMillan.

Richardson, J.T.E. (1992) 'The menstrual cycle, cognition and paramenstrual symptomatology', in J.T.E. Richardson (ed.) *Cognition and the Menstrual Cycle: Culture, Theory and Practice*, London: Springer Verlag, 1–24.

Richey C.A., Gambrill, E.D. and Blythe B.J. (1988) 'Mentor relationships among women in academe', *Affilia: Journal of Women and Social Work*, 3 (1), 34–47.

Riger, S. (1992) 'Epistemological debates, feminist voices: science, social values, and the study of women', *American Psychologist*, 47 (6), 730–740.

Rix, S.E. and Stone, A.J. (1984) 'Work', in S.M. Pritchard (ed.) *The Women's Annual*, Boston: G.K. Hall.

Roazen, P. (1991) *Helene Deutsch: Psychoanalysis of the Sexual Functions of Women*, London: Karnac Books.

Rohrbaugh, J.B. (1981) *Women: Psychology's Puzzle*, Reading: Abacus.

Roiphe, K. (1993) *The Morning After*, London: Vintage.

Rosenberg, J., Perlstadt, H. and Phillips, W.R. (1993) 'Now that we are here: discrimination, disparagement, and harassment at work and the experience of women lawyers', *Gender and Society*, 7 (3), 415–433.

Rossi, A. (1977) 'A biosocial perspective on parenting', *Daedalus*, 106, 1–32.

Sampson, E.E. (1989) 'The deconstruction of the self', in J. Shotter and K.J. Gergen (eds) *Texts of Identity*, London: Sage.

Sanders, C. (1995) 'The Don Juans', *Times Higher Education Supplement*, 10 March, 16–17.

Saussure, F. de (1974) *A Course in General Linguistics*, London: Fontana.

Savage, W. (1986) *A Savage Enquiry: Who Controls Childbirth?*, London: Virago.

Sayers, J. (1982) *Biological Politics*, London: Tavistock.

—— (1986) *Sexual Contradictions*, London: Tavistock.

—— (1992) 'Feminism, psychoanalysis and psychotherapy', in J.M. Ussher and P. Nicolson (eds) *Gender Issues in Clinical Psychology*, London: Routledge.

Segal, L. (1994) *Straight Sex*, London: Virago.

Segal, J. (1992) *Melanie Klein*, London: Sage.

Sheffield University Student Union (1992) *Sexual Harassment Survey*, Sheffield: SUSU.

Sheppard, D. (1989) 'Organisation, power and sexuality: the image and self-image of women managers', in J. Hearn, D.L. Sheppard, P. Tancred-Sheriff and G. Burrell (eds) *The Sexuality of Organisation*, London: Sage.

—— (1992) 'Women managers' perceptions of gender and organisational life', in A.J. Mills and P. Tancred (eds) *Gendering Organisational Analysis*, London: Sage.

Sherif, C. (1987) 'Bias in psychology', in S. Harding (ed.) *Feminism and Methodology*, Milton Keynes: Open University Press.

Shotter, J. (1993) *Cultural Politics of Everyday Life*, Milton Keynes: Open University Press.

Silver, G. (1990) 'Monopoly of middle-aged men' (editorial) *The Lancet*, 335, 1149–1150.

Simpson, S.M. (1990) 'Women entrepreneurs', in J. Firth-Cozens and M.A. West (eds) *Women at Work*, Milton Keynes: Open University Press.

Smith, D.E. (1978) 'A peculiar eclipsing: women's from men's culture', *Women's Studies International Quarterly*, 1, 281–295.

Smith, J.A. (1993) 'Persons, Text and Talk: Subjectivity, Reflexivity and Qualitative Research in Psychology', paper presented at the British Psychological Society's Social Psychology Section Conference, University of Oxford.

Snitow, A., Stansell, C. and Thompson, S. (1984) *Desire: The Politics of Sexuality*, London: Virago.

Sommer, B. (1992) 'Cognitive performance and the menstrual cycle', in J.T.E. Richardson (ed.) *Cognition and the Menstrual Cycle: Research, Theory and Culture*. London: Springer Verlag.

Squire, C. (1990) 'Feminism as "anti psychology"', in E. Burman (ed.) *Feminists in Psychological Practice*, London: Sage.

Stacey, J. (1993) 'Untangling feminist theory', in V. Robinson and D. Richardson (eds) *Introducing Women's Studies*, Basingstoke: Macmillan.

Stanley, L. and Wise, S. (1983) *Breaking Out: Feminist Consciousness and Feminist Research*, London: Routledge and Kegan Paul.

Swan, E. (1994) 'Managing emotion', in M. Tanton (ed.) *Women in Management*, London: Routledge.

Tajfel, H. (ed.) (1978) *Differentiation Between Social Groups: Studies in the Social Psychology of Intergroup Relations*, London: Academic Press.

Tannen, D. (1993) *You Just Don't Understand: Women and Men in Conversation*, London: Virago.

Tanton, M. (1994) *Women in Management*, London: Routledge.

Thom, D. (1992) 'A lop-sided view: feminist history or the history of women?', in K.

Campbell (ed.) *Critical Feminism: Argument in the Disciplines*, Milton Keynes: Open University Press.

Thomas, A.M. (1985) 'The Meaning of Gender in Women's Self-conceptions', paper presented at the British Psychological Society's Social Psychology Section Annual Conference, Clare College, Cambridge.

—— (1986) 'The Personal and the Political in Women's Self-conceptions', paper presented as part of the symposium on Social Factors in Gender Identity held at the British Psychological Society's Annual Conference, University of Sheffield.

Thorne, B. (1986) 'Boys and girls together... but mostly apart: gender arrangements in elementary schools', in W.W. Hartup and Z. Rubin (eds) *Relationships and Development*, Hillsdale, NJ: Erlbaum.

Tunaley, J.R. (1994) 'Young Women, Self and the Thin Ideal, paper presented at the 2nd International Conference on Qualitative Health Research, Pennsylvania State, USA.

—— (1995) 'Body Size, Food and Women's Identity: A Lifespan Approach', unpublished PhD thesis, University of Sheffield.

Unger, R.K. (1979) *Female and Male: Psychological Perspectives*, London: Harper and Row.

Urwin, C. (1984) 'Power relations and emergence of language', in J. Henriques, W. Hollway, C. Urwin, C. Venn and U.V. Walkerdine (eds) *Changing the Subject* London: Methuen.

Ussher, J.M. (1989) *The Psychology of the Female Body*, London: Routledge.

—— (1990a) 'Choosing psychology or not throwing the baby out with the bath water', in E. Burman (ed.) *Feminists and Psychological Practice*, London: Sage.

—— (1990b) 'Sexism in psychology', *The Psychologist*, 13 (9), 31–33.

—— (1991) *Women's Madness: Misogyny or Misunderstanding*, Brighton: Harvester Wheatsheaf.

—— (1992a) 'Science sexing psychology', in J.M. Ussher and P. Nicolson (eds) *Gender Issues in Clinical Psychology*, London: Routledge.

—— (1992b) 'Reproductive rhethoric and the blaming of the body', in P. Nicolson and J.M. Ussher (eds) *The Psychology of Women's Health and Health Care*, Basingstoke: Macmillan.

—— (1993) 'The construction of female sexual problems: regulating sex, regulating women' in J.M. Ussher and C.D. Baker (eds) *Psychological Perspectives on Sexual Problems*, London: Routledge.

—— (1995) 'Masculinity as Masquerade: Deconstructing Phallic Illusions in Pornographic Representation', paper presented at the British Psychological Society's Annual Conference, University of Warwick.

Valverde, M. (1985) *Sex, Power and Pleasure*, Toronto: The Women's Press.

Wager, M. (1995) 'Constructions of Femininity in Academic Women', paper presented at the British Psychological Society's Women and Psychology Annual Conference, University of Leeds.

Walker, A. (1995) 'Theory and methodology in pre-menstrual symptom research', *Social Science and Medicine*, 41 (6), 793–800.

Warner, P. and Walker, A. (1992) 'Editorial: menstrual cycle research – time to take stock', *Journal of Reproductive and Infant Psychology*, 10, 63–66.

Weedon, C. (1987) *Feminist Practice and Poststructuralist Theory*, Oxford: Blackwell.

Weitzman, L. (1979) *Sex Role Socialisation*, Palo Alto, CA: Mayfield.

Wetherell, M. (1993) 'Discussant Paper for Symposium: Subjectivity, Reflexivity and Qualitative Psychology', British Psychological Society's Annual Social Psychology Section Conference, Jesus College, Oxford.

White, B., Cox, C. and Cooper, C. (1992) *Women's Career Development: A Study of High Flyers*, Oxford: Blackwell Business.

Whitford, M. (1993) *The Irigaray Reader*, Oxford: Blackwell.

Wilkinson, S.J. (1986) *Feminist Social Psychology: Theory and Method*, Milton Keynes: Open University Press.

Wilkinson, S.J. (1990) 'Women organising in psychology', in E. Burman (ed.) *Feminists in Psychological Practice*, London: Sage.

Williams, J.A. and Giles, H. (1978) 'The changing status of women in society: an intergroup perspective', in H. Tajfel (ed.) *Differentiation Between Social Groups: Studies in the Social Psychology of Intergroup Relations*, London: Academic Press.

Wilson, E.O. (1978) *On Human Nature*, Cambridge, MA: Harvard University Press.

Wise, S. and Stanley, L. (1987) *Georgie Porgie: Sexual Harrassment in Everyday Life*, London: Pandora.

Witz, A. (1992) *Professions and Patriarchy*, London: Routledge.

—— and Savage (1992) 'The gender of organisations', in M. Savage and A. Witz (eds) *Gender and Bureaucracy*, Oxford: Blackwell.

Wolf, N. (1991) *The Beauty Myth*, London: Vintage.

—— (1994) *Fire with Fire*, London: Vintage.

Woollett, A., Choi, P.Y.L. and Nicolson, P. (1995) 'Teaching Psychology: The Perspective of Women Academic Psychologists', workshop presented at the Women in Psychology Conference, University of Leeds.

# Index

Page numbers in **bold** denote major section/chapter devoted to subject